THE CRISIS
TOPICAL BIBLE

THE CRISIS
TOPICAL BIBLE

Compiled by

SUSAN EAVES

BIBLE VERSIONS
KJ, King James version of the Bible.
NKJV, the New King James Version, Copyright 1982 by Thomas Nelson, Inc.
NLT, Holy Bible, New Living Translation, Copyright 1996, 2004, 2007 by Tyndale House Foundation. All rights reserved.
NIV, trademark of the New International Version. NIV copyright 1973, 1978, 1984 by International Bible Society. Zondervan Publishing House.
AMP, Amplified Bible copyright 1954, 1958, 1962, 1964, 1965, 1987 by the Lockman Foundation.
NCV, New Century Version Copyright 1987, 1988, 1991, By Word Publishing, a division of Thomas Nelson, Inc.

CONTENTS

SPECIAL ACKNOWLEDGEMENTS.. 9
INTRODUCTION.. 13
ADDICTIONS 15
ANXIETY.. 16
BAD NEWS 17
BEING STOLEN FROM... 19
BETRAYAL 20
BONDAGE.. 22
BREAKING BAD HABITS 23
BROKENHEARTED.. 25
CHANGE.. 26
CONCENTRATION 28
CONDEMNATION.. 29
CONFIDENCE 31
CONFUSION.. 32
CONTROL FREAKS... 34
CRISIS.. 35
CRITICISM 37
DEATH... 38
DEPRESSION 40
DESPAIR.. 41
DIFFICULTIES.. 43
DISAPPOINTMENTS 44
DISCERNMENT.. 45
DISCOURAGEMENT 47
DISGRACE... 48
ENEMIES 49
EVIL DOERS... 51

EXHAUSTION 52

FAILURE 54

FALSE ACCUSATIONS 55

FATIGUE 57

FEAR 59

FEAR OF MAN / PEOPLE PLEASING 60

FEAR OF THE LORD 61

FEELING OVERWHELMED 63

FORGIVENESS 64

GOD'S FAITHFULNESS 65

GOD'S FORGIVENESS 67

GOD'S PLANS FOR YOU 68

GOD'S POWER 70

GOD'S UNCONDITIONAL LOVE 71

GUIDANCE 73

HAIR LOSS 74

HIDDEN THINGS 75

HINDERANCES 76

HUMILIATION 78

INSANITY 79

INSUFFICIENT FUNDS 81

JEALOUSY 82

JOB LOSS 83

LEGAL 85

LONELINESS 87

MENTAL WARFARE 88

MISTAKES 90

MOCKERS 91

NEGATIVE EMOTIONS 92

NEGATIVE THOUGHTS 94

OPPRESSION 95

OVERCOMING BITTERNESS 97

OVERCOMING IDOLS 99

OVERCOMING PRIDE 100

OVERCOMING SIN 101

OVERCOMING TEMPTATION 103

OVERCOMING TORMENT 104
PAIN.. 106
PAINFUL MEMORIES 107
PEACE 109
PROBLEM SOLVING 110
PROTECTION... 112
PURPOSE 113
REJECTION.. 115
SECOND CHANCES 116
SECURITY.. 118
SELF HATRED.. 119
SELF-DOUBT 120
SICKNESS 122
SLANDER... 124
SPIRITUAL WARFARE... 125
STRENGTH.. 126
STRESS 128
STRIFE... 130
SUFFERING 131
TERMINAL ILLNESSES / INCURABLE DISEASES............. 133
THE GOD KIND OF LIFE *134*
THE NAME OF THE LORD 136
THE POWER OF A GODLY LIFE 137
THE POWER OF FAITH 139
THE POWER OF FORGIVENESS...................................... 141
THE POWER OF HOPE 142
THE POWER OF OUR WORDS... 144
THE POWER OF PRAYER.. 146
THE POWER OF RIGHT THINKING 147
THE POWER OF THE CROSS... 149
THREATS 151
TRAGEDY 153
TROUBLE 155
UNCERTAINTY.. 156
UNFAIR CIRCUMSTANCES 158
VERBAL ABUSE... 159

VICTORY 161

WEAKNESS.. 162

WEARINESS... 164

WHAT GOD WANTS *YOU TO RECEIVE*............................. 165

WHEN IT SEEMS LIKE YOUR FAITH IS FAILING............. 169

WHEN YOU ARE EMOTIONALLY DRAINED 171

WHEN YOU ARE WOUNDED... 172

WHEN YOU HAVE BLOWN IT.. 173

WHEN YOU NEED HELP FROM HEAVEN 175

WHEN YOU'RE AWAY FROM GOD 177

WHEN YOUR SOUL IS SICK.. 178

WISDOM 180

WORRY 182

TO RECEIVE ETERNAL LIFE.. 184

SUSAN EAVES... 185

SPECIAL ACKNOWLEDGEMENTS

This project became a reality because of the help from many. Special thanks to Anthony Sands who became my hands on this project. Additional thanks to his children who sacrificed time with Dad to finish this project. Thank you to Jo Hock, this would not have happened without your sacrificial giving of time and effort. Thanks to Rickie and Crystal Booth and Robin Art for their additional help. Chris and Chuck Berster, who took frantic phone calls from their technically challenged friend. Leta Perry, who stepped in at the last minute to do the final editing. To my women's Bible study group who helped me with their prayers and encouragement. Thank you to my daughter Genesis who uplifted my spirit with such kind words. Thanks to Kathy Faydash who has been such a wonderful prayer partner for so many years. You are the heroes that made this publication possible!

To My Mom, Anne
Thank you for instilling a love for reading and
learning in all six of your children.
Our lives have been greatly enriched
by your precious gift. Now the lives of countless others
will also be touched and helped
by the gifts you imparted to all of us
so many years ago.
With much love and gratitude,

Susan

INTRODUCTION

If you are reading this book chances are you are in a crisis or know someone going through a crisis. Perhaps every one you know is in crisis and trauma. I have compiled these scriptures based on my own personal experiences with crisis, trauma and heartbreak.

God has helped me to overcome panic attacks, divorce, the death of a child and a horrible car accident. For four very long years I used a motorized wheelchair for anything that required more than a few steps. At times I was unable to use the wheelchair at all because my hands and arms would not cooperate. My hands and feet would pull up into claws and I was left with serious neurological and spinal injuries. The accident came about a year a half after my son's death. I didn't know what hurt more, my body or heartbroken soul.

For many weeks and months I didn't know if I was going to make it. I wanted to lie down on the floor and die, but God faithfully gave me the strength to keep going on. I clung to Him and to the hope His word gave me. I wondered if I would ever be happy again.

I'm overjoyed to tell you that I truly am happy and full of joy. I am a miracle in progress. I now walk most days with a limp, but thanks to God I am walking. Occasionally I still use a wheelchair but this battle is not over until I run again. I miss my son Clint terribly, but I am making new memories and giving hope to others who are hopeless or heartbroken.

Perhaps you have lost a job or a house. You may be severely stressed. Maybe you have lost a loved one or you are experiencing the death of a relationship or marriage. It might be that you have just received the worst doctor's report you have ever had. Possibly you have been living with terrible panic attacks or great depression.

I haven't compiled these scriptures as someone who has arrived. I still face huge challenges but I don't face them alone. You don't have to face your battles alone either.

The one common denominator in all my struggles has been God. He has been with me through every tear cried, each hopeless situation and every crisis. He has given me a strength and grace that I don't possess on my own. He has been faithful when I have not. I have experienced a love and security that is not of this world, they come from heaven.

My purpose in writing this book is to bring heaven's love and security into your life. God does bring purpose out of pain. He gives light in the darkness. He brings order and beauty out of our ruins. How could I not love a God like that?

It is my prayer that this book will help you also and bring you into a closer relationship with the only One who can restore your soul. If you are in crisis read these scriptures and make them more important to you than the air you breathe. God's word is oxygen to your soul. He'll never leave you or forsake you. If you feel like you don't know God please turn to the back of this book to find out how to become His child.

God is a miracle worker and I believe He has a multitude of miracles with your name on them. Please feel free to write me at the address listed in back. The Anchor of Your Soul will make a way for you! I'm believing God with you for miraculous answers to prayer.

With much love,
Susan Eaves

ADDICTIONS

For to be carnally minded is death; but to be spiritually minded is life and peace.

Rom 8:6 KJ

For sin shall not have dominion over you: for ye are not under the law, but under grace.

Rom 6:14 KJ

I have discovered this principle of life—that when I want to do what is right, I inevitably do what is wrong. I love God's law with all my heart. But there is another power within me that is at war with my mind. This power makes me a slave to the sin that is still within me. Oh, what a miserable person I am! Who will free me from this life that is dominated by sin and death? Thank God! The answer is in Jesus Christ our Lord.

Rom 7:21-25 NLT

So now there is no condemnation for those who belong to Christ Jesus. And because you belong to him, the power of the life-giving Spirit has freed you from the power of sin that leads to death.

Ro 8:1-2 NLT

Seeing ye have purified your souls in obeying the truth through the Spirit unto unfeigned love of the brethren, see that ye love one another with a pure heart fervently.

1 Pet 1:22 KJ

Teach me your ways O Lord, that I may live according to your truth! Grant me purity of heart, so that I may honor you.

With all my heart I will praise you, O Lord my God. I will give glory to your name forever, for your love for me is very great.

Ps 86:11-13 NLT

Seeing ye have purified your souls in obeying the truth through the Spirit unto unfeigned love of the brethren, see that ye love one another with a pure heart fervently.

1Pet 1:22 KJ

But Jesus beheld them, and said unto them, with men this is impossible; but with God all things are possible.

Mt 19:26 KJ

ANXIETY

But blessed are those who trust in the Lord and have made the Lord their hope and confidence.

Jer 17:7 NLT

Be still, and know that I am God! I will be honored by every nation. I will be honored throughout the world.

Ps 46:10 NLT

Peace I leave with you, my peace I give unto you: not as the world giveth, give I unto you. Let not your heart be troubled, neither let it be afraid.

Jn 14:27 KJ

Susan Eaves

Thou wilt keep him in perfect peace, whose mind is stayed on thee: because he trusteth in thee. Trust ye in the Lord forever: for in the Lord Jehovah is everlasting strength.

Isa 26:3-4 KJ

Search me, O God, and know my heart; test me and know my anxious thoughts. See if there is any offensive way in me, and lead me in the way everlasting.

Ps 139:23-24 NIV

An anxious heart weighs a man down, but a kind word cheers him up.

Pr 12:25 NIV

The law of his God is in his heart; none of his steps shall slide.

Ps 37:31 KJ

The Lord will perfect that which concerneth me: thy mercy, O Lord, endureth forever.

Ps 138:8 KJ

BAD NEWS

He gives power to the weak and strength to the powerless.

Isa 40:29 NLT

Be sober, be vigilant; because your adversary the devil, as a roaring lion, walketh about, seeking whom he may devour:

1 Pet 5:8 KJ

For every child of God defeats this evil world, and we achieve this victory through our faith. And who can win this battle against the world? Only those who believe that Jesus is the Son of God.

1 Jn 5:4-5 NLT

But Jesus beheld them, and said unto them, With men this is impossible; but with God all things are possible.

Mt 19:26 KJ

Even when there was no reason for hope, Abraham kept hoping believing that he would become the father of many nations.

Rom 4:18 NLT

He will keep you strong to the end so that you will be free from all blame on the day when our Lord Jesus Christ returns.

1 Co 1:8 NLT

Seek the Lord and his strength, seek his face continually.

1 Chr 16:11 KJ

In all their affliction he was afflicted, and the angel of his presence saved them: in his love and in his pity he redeemed them; and he bare them, and carried them all the days of old.

Isa 63:9 KJ

BEING STOLEN FROM

You have allowed me to suffer much hardship, but you will restore me to life again and lift me up from the depths of the earth.

Ps 71:20 NLT

Men do not despise a thief if he steals to satisfy his hunger when he is starving. Yet if he is caught, he must pay sevenfold, though it costs him all the wealth of his house.

Pr 6:30-31 NIV

I will declare the decree: the Lord hath said unto me, Thou art my Son; this day have I begotten thee. Ask of me, and I shall give thee the heathen for thine inheritance, and the uttermost parts of the earth for thy possession.

Ps 2:7-8 KJ

He that followeth after righteousness and mercy findeth life, righteousness, and honour.

Pr 21:21 KJ

Beloved, I wish above all things that thou mayest prosper and be in health, even as thy soul prospereth.

3 Jn:2 KJ

The blessing of the Lord, it maketh rich, and he addeth no sorrow with it.

Pr 10:22 KJ

But thou shalt remember the Lord thy God: for it is he that giveth thee power to get wealth that he may establish his covenant which he sware unto thy fathers, as it is this day.

Deut 8:18 KJ

But my God shall supply all your need according to his riches in glory by Christ Jesus.

Phil 4:19 KJ

O fear the Lord, ye his saints: for there is no want to them that fear him.

Ps 34:9 KJ

BETRAYAL

He will not crush the weakest reed or put out a flickering candle. He will bring justice to all who have been wronged.

Isa 42:3 NLT

And I will deal severely with all who have oppressed you. I will save the weak and helpless ones; I will bring together those who were chased away. I will give glory and fame to my former exiles, wherever they have been mocked and shamed.

Zeph 3:19 NLT

How great is your goodness, which you have stored up for those who fear you, which you bestow in the sight of men on those who take refuge in you. In the shelter of your presence you hide them from the intrigues of men; in your dwelling you keep them safe from accusing tongues.

Ps 31:19-20 NIV

Though I walk in the midst of trouble, thou wilt revive me: thou shalt stretch forth thine hand against the wrath of mine enemies, and thy right hand shall save me.

Ps 138:7 KJ

Though I am surrounded by troubles, you will protect me from the anger of my enemies. You reach out your hand and the power of your right hand saves me. The Lord will work out his plans for my life-for your faithful love, O Lord, endures forever.

Ps 138:7-8 NLT

Who, when he was reviled, reviled not again: when he suffered, he threatened not; but committed himself to him that judgeth righteously.

1 Pet 2:23 KJ

Fear not; you will no longer live in shame. Don't be afraid; there is no more disgrace for you.

Isa 54:4 NLT

Can a woman forget her nursing child? Can she feel no love for the child she has borne? But even if that were possible, I would not forget you! See, I have written your name on the palms of my hands.

Isa 49:15-16 NLT

BONDAGE

"Lord, help!" they cried in their trouble, and he saved them from their distress. He led them from the darkness and deepest gloom; he snapped their chains.

Ps 107:13-14 NLT

In my distress I prayed to the Lord, and the Lord answered me and set me free. The Lord is for me, so I will have no fear. What can mere people do to me?

Ps 118:5-6 NLT

Then said Jesus to those Jews which believed on him, If ye continue in my word, then are ye my disciples indeed; And ye shall know the truth, and the truth shall make you free.

Jn 8:31-32 KJ

During that long period, the king of Egypt died. The Israelites groaned in their slavery and cried out, and their cry for help because of their slavery went up to God. God heard their groaning and he remembered his covenant with Abraham, with Isaac and with Jacob.

Ex 2:23-24 NIV

Behold, God is mine helper: the Lord is with them that uphold my soul.

Ps 54:4 KJ

No weapon that is formed against thee shall prosper; and every tongue that shall rise against thee in judgment thou shalt condemn. This is the heritage of the servants of the Lord, and their righteousness is of me, saith the Lord.

Isa 54:17 KJ

The Lord is good to those whose hope is in him, to the one who seeks him.

Lam 3:25 NIV

But you, O Lord are a God of compassion and mercy, slow to get angry and filled with unfailing love and faithfulness. Look down and have mercy on me. Give your strength to your servant.

Ps 86:15-16 NLT

For ye were as sheep going astray; but are now returned unto the Shepherd and Bishop of your souls.

1Pet 2:25 KJ

BREAKING BAD HABITS

Wherewithal shall a young man cleanse his way? by taking heed thereto according to thy word.

Ps 119:9 KJ

By mercy and truth iniquity is purged: and by the fear of the Lord men depart from evil.

Pr 16:6 KJ

And with all deceivableness of unrighteousness in them that perish; because they received not the love of the truth, that they might be saved.

2 Th 2:10 KJ

Let my supplication come before thee: deliver me according to thy word.

Ps 119:170 KJ

O Lord my God, I cried unto thee, and thou hast healed me.

Ps 30:2 KJ

For he hath not despised nor abhorred the affliction of the afflicted; neither hath he hid his face from him; but when he cried unto him, he heard.

Ps 22:24 KJ

During that long period, the king of Egypt died. The Israelites groaned in their slavery and cried out, and their cry for help because of their slavery went up to God. God heard their groaning and he remembered his covenant with Abraham, with Isaac and with Jacob.

Ex 2:23-24 NIV

Those who pay regard to false, useless, and worthless idols forsake their own (Source of) mercy and loving-kindness.

Jonah 2:8 AMP

He that hath no rule over his own spirit is like a city that is broken down, and without walls.

Pr 25:28 KJ

BROKENHEARTED

He healeth the broken in heart, and bindeth up their wounds.

Ps 147:3 KJ

The Lord is close to the brokenhearted; he rescues those whose spirits are crushed.

Ps 34:18 NLT

The sacrifice you desire is a broken spirit. You will not reject a broken and repentant heart, O God.

Ps 51:17 NLT

Peace I leave with you, my peace I give unto you: not as the world giveth, give I unto you. Let not your heart be troubled, neither let it be afraid.

Jn 14:27 KJ

The Spirit of the Lord God is upon me; because the Lord hath anointed me to preach good tidings unto the meek; he hath sent me to bind up the brokenhearted, to proclaim liberty to the captives, and the opening of the prison to them that are bound; To proclaim the acceptable year of the Lord, and the day of vengeance of our God; to comfort all that mourn; To appoint unto them that mourn in Zion, to give unto them beauty for ashes, the oil of joy for mourning, the garment of praise for the spirit of heaviness; that they might be called trees of righteousness, the planting of the Lord, that he might be glorified.

Isa 61:1-3 KJ

I will search for my lost ones who strayed away, and I will bring them safely home again. I will bandage the injured and strengthen the weak. But I will destroy those who are fat and powerful. I will feed them, yes - feed them justice!

Ezek 34:16 NLT

Though a host should encamp against me, my heart shall not fear: though war should rise against me, in this will I be confident.

Ps 27:3 KJ

CHANGE

When you go through deep waters, I will be with you. When you go through rivers of difficulty, you will not drown. When you walk through the fire of oppression, you will not be burned up; the flames will not consume you.

Isa 43:2 NLT

I will go before thee, and make the crooked places straight: I will break in pieces the gates of brass, and cut in sunder the bars of iron.

Isa 45:2 KJ

Your word, O Lord, is eternal; it stands firm in the heavens.

Ps 119:89 NIV

Jesus Christ the same yesterday, and today, and forever.

Heb 13:8 KJ

For I am the Lord, I change not.

Mal 3:6 KJ

He did not waver at the promise of God through unbelief, but was strengthened in faith, giving glory to God, and being fully convinced that what he had promised he was also able to perform.

Rom 4:20-21 NKJ

I will be glad and rejoice in thy mercy; for thou hast considered my trouble; thou hast known my soul in adversities.

Ps 31:7 KJ

Cast thy burden upon the Lord, and he shall sustain thee; he shall never suffer the righteous to be moved.

Ps 55:22 KJ

In all thy ways acknowledge him, and he shall direct thy paths.

Pr 3:6 KJ

Come unto me, all ye that labour and are heavy laden and I will give you rest.

Mt 11:28 KJ

Be still, and know that I am God.

Ps 46:10 KJ

CONCENTRATION

I will pursue your commands, for you expand my understanding.

Ps 119:32 NLT

Confounded be all they that serve graven images that boast themselves of idols.

Ps 97:7 KJ

For the Lord God will help me; therefore shall I not be confounded: therefore have I set my face like a flint, and I know that I shall not be ashamed.

Isa 50:7 KJ

Through these he has given us his very great and precious promises, so that through them you may participate in the divine nature and escape the corruption in the world caused by evil desires.

2 Pet 1:4 NIV

Blessed is the man who perseveres under trial, because when he has stood the test, he will receive the crown of life that God has promised to those who love him.

Ja 1:12 NIV

Be self-controlled and alert. Your enemy the devil prowls around like a roaring lion looking for someone to devour. Resist him, standing firm in the faith, because you know that your brothers throughout the world are undergoing the same kind of sufferings.

1 Pe 5:8-9 NIV

But the manifestation of the Spirit is given to every man to profit withal.

1 Cor 12:7 KJ

If any of you lack wisdom, let him ask of God, that giveth to all men liberally, and upbraideth not; and it shall be given him.

James 1:5 KJ

In him we have redemption through his blood, the forgiveness of sins, in accordance with the riches of God's grace that he lavished on us with all wisdom and understanding. And he made known to us the mystery of his will according to his good pleasure, which he purposed in Christ.

Eph 1:7-9 NIV

CONDEMNATION

The Lord redeems his servants; no one will be condemned who takes refuge in him.

Ps 34:22 NIV

And this is the confidence that we have in him, that, if we ask any thing according to his will, he heareth us:

1 Jn 5:14 KJ

Therefore [there is] now no condemnation (no adjudging guilty of wrong) for those who are in Christ Jesus, who live [and] walk not after the dictates of the flesh, but after the dictates of the Spirit. For the law of the Spirit of life [which is] in Christ Jesus [the law of our new being] has freed me from the law of sin and of death.

Rom 8:1-2 AMP

To the praise of the glory of his grace, wherein he hath made us accepted in the beloved. In whom we have redemption through his blood, the forgiveness of sins, according to the riches of his grace;

Eph 1:6-7 KJ

Therefore, since we have been made right in God's sight by faith, we have peace with God because of what Jesus Christ our Lord has done for us.

Rom 5:1 NLT

For what the law could not do, in that it was weak through the flesh, God sending his own Son in the likeness of sinful flesh, and for sin, condemned sin in the flesh:

Rom 8:3 KJ

There is therefore now no condemnation to them which are in Christ Jesus, who walk not after the flesh, but after the Spirit.

Rom 8:1 KJ

Thou wilt keep him in perfect peace, whose mind is stayed on thee: because he trusteth in thee.

Isa 26:3 KJ

For God sent not his Son into the world to condemn the world; but that the world through him might be saved. He that believeth on him is not condemned: but he that believeth not is condemned already, because he hath not believed in the name of the only begotten Son of God.

Jn 3:17-18 KJ

CONFIDENCE

It is better to take refuge in the Lord than to trust in man.

Ps 118:8 NIV

The Lord is my light and my salvation; whom shall I fear? the Lord is the strength of my life; of whom shall I be afraid?

Ps 27:1 KJ

Fear thou not; for I am with thee: be not dismayed; for I am thy God: I will strengthen thee; yea, I will help thee; yea, I will uphold thee with the right hand of my righteousness.

Isa 41:10 KJ

I sought the Lord, and he heard me, and delivered me from all my fears.

Ps 34:4 KJ

And this is the confidence that we have in him that, if we ask any thing according to his will, he heareth us: And if we know that he hear us, whatsoever we ask, we know that we have the petitions that we desired of him.

1 Jn 5:14-15 KJ

Who is he that condemneth? It is Christ that died, yea rather, that is risen again, who is even at the right hand of God, who also maketh intercession for us.

Rom 8:34 KJ

Which hope we have as an anchor of the soul, both sure and stedfast, and which entereth into that within the veil.

Heb 6:19 KJ

Call unto me, and I will answer thee, and show thee great and mighty things, which thou knowest not.

Jer 33:3 KJ

He that handleth a matter wisely shall find good: and whoso trusteth in the Lord, happy is he.

Pr 16:20 KJ

CONFUSION

In thee, O Lord, do I put my trust: let me never be put to confusion.

Ps 71:1 KJ

For the Lord God will help me; therefore shall I not be confounded: therefore have I set my face like a flint, and I know that I shall not be ashamed.

Isa 50:7 KJ

Thus saith the Lord, the Holy One of Israel, and his Maker, Ask me of things to come concerning my sons, and concerning the work of my hands command ye me.

Isa 45:11 KJ

They cried out to you and were saved. They trusted in you and were never disgraced.

Ps 22:5 NLT

All the paths of the Lord are mercy and truth unto such as keep his covenant and his testimonies.

Ps 25:10 KJ

Show me the right path, O Lord; point out the road for me to follow.

Ps 25:4 NLT

For where envying and strife is, there is confusion and every evil work.

James 3:16 KJ

But Israel shall be saved by the Lord with an everlasting salvation: You shall not be ashamed or disgraced.

Isa 45:17 NKJ

For God is not the author of confusion, but of peace.

1 Cor 14:33 NLT

And it shall come to pass in the day that the Lord shall give thee rest from thy sorrow, and from thy fear, and from the hard bondage wherein thou wast made to serve.

Isa 14:3 NKJ

CONTROL FREAKS

As pressure and stress bear down on me, I find joy in your commands.

Ps 119:143 NLT

Argue my case; take my side! Protect my life as you promised.

Ps 119:154 NLT

You intended to harm me, but God intended it for good to accomplish what is now being done, the saving of many lives.

Gen 50:20 NIV

But if thou shalt indeed obey his voice, and do all that I speak; then I will be an enemy unto thine enemies, and an adversary unto thine adversaries.

Ex 23:22 KJ

But thus saith the Lord, Even the captives of the mighty shall be taken away, and the prey of the terrible shall be delivered: for I will contend with him that contendeth with thee, and I will save thy children.

Isa 49:25 KJ

The Lord taketh my part with them that help me: therefore shall I see my desire upon them that hate me.

Ps 118:7 KJ

Be strong and courageous, be not afraid nor dismayed for the king of Assyria, nor for all the multitude that is with him: for there be more with us than with him: With him is an arm of flesh; but with us is the Lord our God to help us, and to fight our battles. And the people rested themselves upon the words of Hezekiah king of Judah.

2 Ch 32:7-8 KJ

The unjust tyrant shall reap disaster and his reign of terror shall end.

Pr 22:8 LB

Drive out the scoffer, and contention will go out; yes, strife and abuse will cease.

Pr 22:10 AMP

The eyes of the Lord preserve knowledge, and he overthroweth the words of the transgressor.

Pr 22:12 KJ

CRISIS

The eternal God is your refuge, and his everlasting arms are under you. He drives out the enemy before you; he cries out, 'Destroy them!'

Deut 33:27 NLT

He grants the desires of those who fear him; he hears their cries for help and rescues them.

Ps 145:19 NLT

As a father has compassion on his children, so the Lord has compassion on those who fear him.

Ps 103:13 NIV

In God, whose word I praise, in God I trust; I will not be afraid. What can mortal man do to me?

Ps 56:4 NIV

And do not grumble, as some of them did - and were killed by the destroying angel.

1 Cor 10:10 NIV

I complained, and my spirit was overwhelmed within me.

Ps 77:3 KJ

O Lord, you are so good, so ready to forgive, so full of unfailing love for all who ask for your help.

Ps 86:5 NLT

The righteous person faces many troubles, but the Lord comes to the rescue each time.

Ps 34:19 NLT

For the Lord your God is the one who goes with you to fight for you against your enemies to give you victory.

Deut 20:4 NIV

The Lord gave David victory wherever he went.

2 Sam 8:6 NLT

CRITICISM

It is better to trust in the Lord than to put confidence in man. It is better to trust in the Lord than to put confidence in princes.

Ps 118:8-9 KJ

For God sent not his Son into the world to condemn the world; but that the world through him might be saved.

Jn 3:17 KJ

For every one that doeth evil hateth the light, neither cometh to the light, lest his deeds should be reproved. But he that doeth truth cometh to the light, that his deeds may be made manifest, that they are wrought in God.

Jn 3:20-21 KJ

In the fear of the Lord is strong confidence: and his children shall have a place of refuge.

Pr 14:26 KJ

Being confident of this very thing, that he which hath begun a good work in you will perform it until the day of Jesus Christ.

Phil 1:6 KJ

Godly people find life; evil people find death.

Pr 11:19 NLT

When pride cometh, then cometh shame: but with the lowly is wisdom.

Pr 11:2 KJ

Blessed (happy, to be envied, and spiritually prosperous--with life-joy and satisfaction in God's favor and salvation, regardless of your outward conditions) are you when people revile you and persecute you and say all kinds of evil things against you falsely on My account.

Mt 5:11 AMP

But the wisdom that comes from heaven is first of all pure; then peace-loving, considerate, submissive, full of mercy and good fruit, impartial and sincere. Peacemakers who sow in peace raise a harvest of righteousness.

Ja 3:17-18 NIV

DEATH

To all who mourn in Israel, he will give a crown of beauty for ashes, a joyous blessing instead of mourning, festive praise instead of despair. In their righteousness, they will be like great oaks that the Lord has planted for his own glory.

Isa 61:3 NLT

Forasmuch then as the children are partakers of flesh and blood, he also himself likewise took part of the same; that through death he might destroy him that had the power of death, that is, the devil.

Heb 2:14 KJ

Jesus said unto her, I am the resurrection, and the life: he that believeth in me, though he were dead, yet shall he live: And whosoever liveth and believeth in me shall never die. Believest thou this?

Jn 11:25-26 KJ

So when this corruptible shall have put on incorruption, and this mortal shall have put on immortality, then shall be brought to pass the saying that is written, Death is swallowed up in victory. O death, where is thy sting? O grave, where is thy victory? The sting of death is sin; and the strength of sin is the law. But thanks be to God, which giveth us the victory through our Lord Jesus Christ.

1 Cor 15:54-57 KJ

Thy sun shall no more go down; neither shall thy moon withdraw itself: for the Lord shall be thine everlasting light, and the days of thy mourning shall be ended.

Isa 60:20 KJ

The Lord is good, a strong hold in the day of trouble; and he knoweth them that trust in him.

Nah 1:7 KJ

Blessed be God, even the Father of our Lord Jesus Christ, the Father of mercies, and the God of all comfort; Who comforteth us in all our tribulation, that we may be able to comfort them which are in any trouble, by the comfort wherewith we ourselves are comforted of God.

2 Cor 1:3-4 KJ

Yea, though I walk through the valley of the shadow of death, I will fear no evil: for thou are with me; they rod and thy staff they comfort me.

Ps 23:4 KJ

There remaineth therefore a rest to the people of God.

Heb 4:9 KJ

Now the Lord of peace himself give you peace always by all means. The Lord be with you all.

2 Thess 3:16 KJ

DEPRESSION

The unfolding of your words gives light; it gives understanding to the simple.

Ps 119:130 NIV

You will surely forget your trouble, recalling it only as waters gone by. Life will be brighter than noonday, and darkness will become like morning.

Job 11:16-17 NIV

And call upon me in the day of trouble: I will deliver thee, and thou shalt glorify me.

Ps 50:15 KJ

By this I know that you are well pleased with me, because my enemy does not triumph over me.

Ps 41:11 KJ

Then they cry unto the Lord in their trouble, and he saveth them out of their distresses.

Ps 107:19 KJ

Weeping may endure for a night, but joy cometh in the morning.

Ps 30:5 KJ

To appoint unto them that mourn in Zion, to give unto them beauty for ashes, the oil of joy for mourning, the garment of praise for the spirit of heaviness.

Isa 61:3 KJ

When thou passest through the waters, I will be with thee; and through the rivers, they shall not overflow thee: when thou walkest through the fire, thou shalt not be burned; neither shall the flame kindle upon thee.

Isa 43:2 KJ

DESPAIR

Tell the godly that all will be well for them. They will enjoy the rich reward they have earned!

Isa 3:10 NLT

In that day the people will proclaim, "This is our God! We trusted in him, and he saved us! This is the Lord, in whom we trusted. Let us rejoice in the salvation he brings!"

Isa 25:9 NLT

There hath no temptation taken you but such as is common to man: but God is faithful, who will not suffer you to be tempted above that ye are able; but will with the temptation also make a way to escape, that ye may be able to bear it.

1 Cor 10:13 KJ

He is the Rock, his work is perfect: for all his ways are judgment: a God of truth and without iniquity, just and right is he.

Deut 32:4 KJ

Your kingdom is an everlasting kingdom, and your dominion endures through all generations. The Lord is faithful to all his promises and loving toward all he has made.

Ps 145:13 NIV

But the wisdom that is from above is first pure, then peaceable, gentle, and easy to be intreated, full of mercy and good fruits, without partiality, and without hypocrisy.

Ja 3:17 KJ

Thou hast also given me the shield of thy salvation: and thy right hand hath holden me up, and thy gentleness hath made me great.

Ps 18:35 KJ

And the Lord shall deliver me from every evil work, and will preserve me unto his heavenly kingdom.

2 Tim 4:18 KJ

DIFFICULTIES

And to whom was God speaking when he took an oath that they would never enter his rest? Wasn't it the people who disobeyed him? So we see that because of their unbelief they were not able to enter his rest.

Heb 3:18-19 NLT

When you go through deep waters, I will be with you. When you go through rivers of difficulty, you will not drown. When you walk through the fire of oppression, you will not be burned up; the flames will not consume you.

Isa 43:2 NLT

To give light to them that sit in darkness and in the shadow of death, to guide our feet into the way of peace.

Lk 1:79 KJ

That the communication of thy faith may become effectual by the acknowledging of every good thing which is in you in Christ Jesus.

Phm 1:6 KJ

And I will be found of you, saith the Lord: and I will turn away your captivity.

Jer 29:14 KJ

For now we live, if ye stand fast in the Lord.

1 Th 3:8 KJ

So the Lord must wait for you to come to him so he can show you his love and compassion. For the Lord is a faithful God. Blessed are those who wait for his help.

Isa 30:18 NLT

Which hope we have as an anchor of the soul, both sure and stedfast, and which entereth into that within the veil.

Heb 6:19 KJ

DISAPPOINTMENTS

When doubts filled my mind, your comfort gave me renewed hope and cheer.

Ps 94:19 NLT

My God, rescue me from the power of the wicked, from the clutches of cruel oppressors.

Ps 71:4 NLT

They cried to you and were saved; in you they trusted and were not disappointed.

Ps 22:5 NIV

Then you will know that I am the Lord; those who hope in me will not be disappointed.

Isa 49:23 NIV

And if it seem evil unto you to serve the Lord, choose you this day whom ye will serve whether the gods which your fathers served that were on the other side of the flood, or the gods of the Amorites, in whose land ye dwell: but as for me and my house, we will serve the Lord.

Josh 24:15 KJ

He cared for them with a true heart and led them with skillful hands.

Ps 78:72 NLT

For he does not enjoy hurting people or causing them sorrow.

Lam 3:33 NLT

And hope does not disappoint us, because God has poured out his love into our hearts by the Holy Spirit, whom he has given us. You see at just the right time, when we were still powerless, Christ died for the ungodly.

Rom 5:5-6 NIV

DISCERNMENT

Daniel answered and said, Blessed be the name of God for ever and ever: for wisdom and might are his: And he changeth the times and the seasons: he removeth kings, and setteth up kings: he giveth wisdom unto the wise, and knowledge to them that know understanding: He revealeth the deep and secret things: he knoweth what is in the darkness, and the light dwelleth with him.

Dan 2:20-22 KJ

But there is a God in heaven that revealeth secrets, and maketh known to the king Nebuchadnezzar what shall be in the latter days.

Dan 2:28 KJ

Howbeit when he, the Spirit of truth, is come, he will guide you into all truth: for he shall not speak of himself; but whatsoever he shall hear, that shall he speak: and he will shew you things to come. He shall glorify me: for he shall receive of mine, and shall shew it unto you.

Jn 16:13-14 KJ

But God hath revealed them unto us by his Spirit: for the Spirit searcheth all things, yea, the deep things of God.

1 Cor 2:10 KJ

Look beneath the surface so you can judge correctly.

Jn 7:24 NLT

My sheep hear my voice, and I know them, and they follow me.

Jn 10:27 KJ

Be sober, be vigilant; because your adversary the devil, as a roaring lion, walketh about, seeking whom he may devour: Whom resist stedfast in the faith, knowing that the same afflictions are accomplished in your brethren that are in the world.

1Pet 5:8-9 KJ

DISCOURAGEMENT

Great is his faithfulness; his mercies begin afresh each morning.

Lam 3:23 NLT

So the Lord must wait for you to come to him so he can show you his love and compassion. For the Lord is a faithful God. Blessed are those who wait for his help.

Isa 30:18 NLT

Have I not commanded you? Be strong and courageous. Do not be terrified; do not be discouraged, for the Lord your God will be with you wherever you go.

Josh 1:9 NIV

Be strong and courageous, and do the work. Do not be afraid or discouraged, for the Lord God, my God is with you. He will not fail you or forsake you until all the work for the service of the temple of the Lord is finished.

1 Chr 28:20 NIV

He said: "Listen, King Jehoshaphat and all who live in Judah and Jerusalem! This is what the Lord says to you: 'Do not be afraid or discouraged because of this vast army. For the battle is not yours, but God's."

2 Chr 20:15 NIV

Now I will take the load from your shoulders; I will free your hands from their heavy tasks. You cried to me in trouble, and I saved you.

Ps 81: 6-7 NLT

I say to myself, "The Lord is my inheritance; therefore, I will hope in him!" The Lord is good to those who depend on him, to those who search for him. So it is good to wait quietly for salvation from the Lord.

Lam 3:24-26 NLT

Be not overcome of evil, but overcome evil with good.

Rom 12:21 KJ

DISGRACE

As the Scriptures say, I am placing a cornerstone in Jerusalem, chosen for great honor, and anyone who trusts in him will never be disgraced.

1 Pet 2:6 NLT

Day by day the Lord takes care of the innocent, and they will receive an inheritance that lasts forever. They will not be disgraced in hard times; even in famine they will have more than enough.

Ps 37:18-19 NLT

Your commands make me wiser than my enemies, for they are my constant guide.

Ps 119:98 NLT

Fear not; you will no longer live in shame. Don't be afraid; there is no more disgrace for you. You will no longer remember the shame of your youth and the sorrows of widowhood.

Isa 54:4 NLT

For the eyes of the Lord are over the righteous, and his ears are open unto their prayers: but the face of the Lord is against them that do evil.

1 Pet 3:12 KJ

The Lord redeemeth the soul of his servants: and none of them that trust in him shall be desolate.

Ps 34:22 KJ

But whoso hearkens to me [Wisdom] shall dwell securely and in confident trust and shall be quiet, without fear or dread of evil.

Pr 1:33 AMP

Then I acknowledged my sin to you and did not cover up my iniquity. I said, "I will confess my transgressions to the Lord and you forgave the guilt of my sin."

Ps 32:5-7 NIV

ENEMIES

What shall we then say to these things? If God be for us, who can be against us?

Rom 8:31 KJ

O Lord, I have so many enemies; so many are against me. So many are saying, "God will never rescue him!" But you, O Lord, are a shield around me; you are my glory, the one who holds my head high.

Ps 3:1-3 NLT

He that spared not his own Son, but delivered him up for us all, how shall he not with him also freely give us all things?

Rom 8:32 KJ

Offer unto God thanksgiving; and pay thy vows unto the most High: And call upon me in the day of trouble: I will deliver thee, and thou shalt glorify me.

Ps 50:14-15 KJ

Who can snatch the plunder of war from the hands of a warrior? Who can demand that a tyrant let his captives go? But the Lord says, The captives of warriors will be released, and the plunder of tyrants will be retrieved. For I will fight those who fight you, and I will save your children.

Isa 49:24-26 NLT

Nay, in all these things we are more than conquerors through him that loved us.

Rom 8:37 KJ

Who shall lay any thing to the charge of God's elect? It is God that justifieth.

Rom 8:33 KJ

So that we may boldly say, The Lord is my helper, and I will not fear what man shall do unto me.

Heb 13:6 KJ

The wicked draw their swords and string their bows to kill the poor and the oppressed, to slaughter those who do right. But their swords will stab their own hearts, and their bows will be broken.

Ps 37:14-15 NLT

EVIL DOERS

Say to those with fearful hearts, "Be strong, and do not fear, for your God is coming to destroy your enemies. He is coming to save you."

Isa 35:4 NLT

Contend, O Lord, with those who contend with me; fight against those who fight against me.

Ps 35:1 NIV

But when the plot came to the king's attention, he issued written orders that the evil scheme Haman had devised against the Jews should come back onto his own head, and that he and his sons should be hanged on the gallows.

Es 9:25 NIV

All my enemies will be ashamed and dismayed; they will turn back in sudden disgrace.

Ps 6:10 NIV

Though they plot evil against you and devise wicked schemes, they cannot succeed.

Ps 21:11 NIV

For evildoers shall be cut off: but those that wait upon the Lord, they shall inherit the earth.

Ps 37:9 KJ

Fret not thyself because of evildoers, neither be thou envious against the workers of iniquity. For they shall soon be cut down like the grass, and wither as the green herb.

Ps 37:1-2 KJ

My God, rescue me from the power of the wicked, from the clutches of cruel oppressors.

Ps 71:4 NLT

He is the God who pays back those who harm me: he brings down the nations under me and delivers me from my enemies. You hold me safe beyond the reach of my enemies; you save me from violent opponents.

2 Sam 22:48-49 NLT

EXHAUSTION

Come to me, all of you who are weary and carry heavy burdens, and I will give you rest. Take my yoke upon you. Let me teach you, because I am humble and gentle of heart, and you will find rest for your souls.

Mt 11:28-29 NLB

This is what the Lord says: Stop at the crossroads and look around. Ask for the old, godly way, and walk in it. Travel its path, and you will find rest for your souls.

Jer 6:16 NLB

Let my soul be at rest again, for the Lord has been good to me. He has saved me from death, my eyes from tears, my feet from stumbling.

Ps 116:7-8 NLT

In my distress I prayed to the Lord and the Lord answered me and set me free. The Lord is for me, so I will have no fear. What can mere people do to me? Yes, the Lord is for me; he will help me. I will look in triumph at those who hate me.

Ps 118:5-7 NLT

Come to me, all you who labor and are heavy laden, and I will give you rest. Take my yoke upon you and learn from me, for I am gentle and lowly in heart, and you will find rest for your souls for my yoke is easy and my burden is light.

Mt 11:28-30 KJ

For I have satiated the weary soul, and I have replenished every sorrowful soul.

Jer 31:25 KJ

Not by might, nor be power, but by my spirit saith the Lord of hosts.

Zech 4:6 KJ

Be strong and of a good courage, fear not, nor be afraid of them; for the Lord thy God, he it is that doth go with thee; he will not fail thee, nor forsake thee.

Deu 31:6 KJ

And God is able to make all grace abound toward you; that ye, always having all sufficiency in all things, may abound to every good work.

2 Cor 9:8 KJ

Call unto me, and I will answer thee, and shew thee great and mighty things, which thou knowest not.

Jer 33:3 KJ

FAILURE

Let, I pray thee, thy merciful kindness be for my comfort, according to thy word unto thy servant. Let thy tender mercies come unto me, that I may live: for thy law is my delight.

Ps 119:76-77 KJ

But if the wicked will turn from all his sins that he hath committed, and keep all my statutes, and do that which is lawful and right, he shall surely live, he shall not die. All his transgressions that he hath committed, they shall not be mentioned unto him: in his righteousness that he hath done he shall live.

Ezek 18:21-22 KJ

I can do all things through Christ which strengtheneth me.

Phil 4:13 KJ

He shall not be afraid of evil tidings; his heart is firmly fixed, trusting (leaning on and being confident) in the Lord. His heart is established and steady, he will not be afraid while he waits to see his desire established upon his adversaries.

Ps 112:7-8 AMP

Yes, the Lord is for me; he will help me. I will look in triumph at those who hate me.

Ps 118:7 NLT

Only be thou strong and very courageous, that thou mayest observe to do according to all the law, which Moses my servant commanded thee: turn not from it to the right hand or to the left, that thou mayest prosper withersoever thou goest.

Josh 1:7 KJ

The Lord upholdeth all that fall, and raiseth up all those that be bowed down.

Ps 145:14 KJ

FALSE ACCUSATIONS

And Jesus said unto them, Because of your unbelief: for verily I say unto you, If ye have faith as a grain of mustard seed, ye shall say unto this mountain, Remove hence to yonder place; and it shall remove; and nothing shall be impossible unto you.

Mt 17:20 KJ

Let them be confounded and consumed that are adversaries to my soul; let them be covered with reproach and dishonour that seek my hurt.

Ps 71:13 KJ

Let mine adversaries be clothed with shame, and let them cover themselves with their own confusion, as with a mantle.

Ps 109:29 KJ

Surround me with your tender mercies so I may live, for your instructions are my delight. Bring disgrace upon the arrogant people who lied about me; meanwhile, I will concentrate on your commandments.

Ps 71:13 NCV

Joyful are people of integrity, who follow the instructions of the Lord.

Ps 119:1 NLT

Wherefore take unto you the whole armour of God, that ye may be able to withstand in the evil day, and having done all, to stand.

Eph 6:13 KJ

For we are not fighting against flesh-and-blood enemies, but against evil rulers and authorities of the unseen world, against mighty powers in this dark world, and against evil spirits in the heavenly places.

Eph 6:12 NLT

Therefore, the proud may not stand in your presence, for you hate all who do evil.

Ps 5:5 NLT

Finally, my brethren, be strong in the Lord, and in the power of his might.

Eph 6:10 KJ

And the God of peace shall bruise Satan under your feet shortly. The grace of our Lord Jesus Christ be with you. Amen.

Ro 16:20 KJ

FATIGUE

Then Jesus said, "Come to me, all of you who are weary and carry heavy burdens, and I will give you rest. Take my yoke upon you. Let me teach you, because I am humble and gentle at heart, and you will find rest for your souls."

Mt 11:28-29 NLT

He giveth power to the faint; and to them that have no might he increaseth strength. Even the youths shall faint and be weary, and the young men shall utterly fall: But they that wait upon the Lord shall renew their strength; they shall mount up with wings as eagles; they shall run, and not be weary; and they shall walk, and not faint.

Isa 40:29-31 KJ

The people will declare, "The Lord is the source of all my righteousness and strength." And all who were angry with him will come to him and be ashamed.

Isa 45:24 NLT

But He said to me, My grace (My favor and loving-kindness and mercy) is enough for you [sufficient against any danger and enables you to bear the trouble manfully]; for My strength and power are made perfect (fulfilled and completed) and show themselves most effective in [your] weakness. Therefore, I will all the more gladly glory in my weaknesses and infirmities, that the strength and power of Christ (the Messiah) may rest (yes, may pitch a tent over and dwell) upon me!

2 Cor 12:9 AMP

Wherefore seeing we also are compassed about with so great a cloud of witnesses, let us lay aside every weight, and the sin which doth so easily beset us, and let us run with patience the race that is set before us, Looking unto Jesus the author and finisher of our faith; who for the joy that was set before him endured the cross, despising the shame, and is set down at the right hand of the throne of God.

Heb 12:1-2 KJ

Dear friend, I hope all is well with you and that you are as healthy in body as you are strong in spirit.

3 Jn 1:2 NLT

Susan Eaves

FEAR

For God has not given us the spirit of fear; but of power, and of love, and of a sound mind.

2 Tim 1:7 KJ

After these things the word of the Lord came unto Abram in a vision, saying, Fear not, Abram: I am thy shield, and thy exceeding great reward.

Gen 15:1 KJ

And he answered, Fear not: for they that be with us are more than they that be with them.

2 Ki 6:16 KJ

Ye shall not need to fight in this battle: set yourselves, stand ye still, and see the salvation of the Lord with you, O Judah and Jerusalem: fear not, nor be dismayed; to morrow go out against them: for the Lord will be with you.

2 Chr 20:17 KJ

On that day they will say to Jerusalem, Do not fear O Zion; and to Zion, do not let not your hands hang limp. The Lord your God is with you, he is mighty to save. He will take great delight in you, he will quiet you with his love, he will rejoice over you with singing.

Zeph 3:16-17 KJ

There is no fear in love; but perfect love cast out fear, because fear involves torment. But he who fears has not been made perfect in love.

1 Jn 4:18 NKJ

Such love has no fear, because perfect love expels all fear. If we are afraid, it is for fear of punishment, and this shows that we have not fully experienced his perfect love. We love each other because he loved us first.

1 Jn 4:18-19 NLT

The fear of man brings a snare, but whoever trusts in the Lord shall be safe.

Pr 29:25 NKJ

FEAR OF MAN / PEOPLE PLEASING

The Lord is for me, so I will have no fear. What can mere people do to me?

Ps 118:6 NLT

A man that flattereth his neighbour spreadeth a net for his feet.

Pr 29:5 KJ

Hear me, you who know what is right, you people who have my law in your hearts: Do not fear the reproach of men or be terrified by their insults.

Isa 51:7 NIV

In God have I put my trust: I will not be afraid what man can do unto me.

Ps 56:11 KJ

For ye have not received the spirit of bondage again to fear; but ye have received the Spirit of adoption, whereby we cry, Abba, Father.

Rom 8:15 KJ

For God hath not given us the spirit of fear; but of power, and of love, and of a sound mind.

2 Tim 1:7 KJ

For what is a man profited, if he shall gain the whole world, and lose his own soul? or what shall a man give in exchange for his soul?

Mt 16:26 KJ

But if thou shalt indeed obey his voice, and do all that I speak; then I will be an enemy unto thine enemies, and an adversary unto thine adversaries.

Ex 23:22 KJ

FEAR OF THE LORD

To fear the Lord means to reverence him.

The Lord is a friend to those who fear him. He teaches them his covenant.

Ps 25:14 NLT

So shall they fear the name of the Lord from the west, and his glory from the rising of the sun. When the enemy shall come in like a flood, the Spirit of the Lord shall lift up a standard against him.

Isa 59:19 KJ

But unto you that fear my name shall the Sun of righteousness arise with healing in his wings; and ye shall go forth, and grow up as calves of the stall.

Mal 4:2 KJ

The Lord taketh pleasure in them that fear him, in those that hope in his mercy.

Ps 147:11 KJ

Only fear the Lord, and serve him in truth with all your heart: for consider how great things he hath done for you.

1 Sam 12:24 KJ

The fear of the Lord is the beginning of knowledge.

Pr 1:7 KJ

The fear of the Lord is strong confidence: and his children shall have a place of refuge.

Pr 14:26 KJ

O How great is thy goodness, which thou hast laid up for them that fear thee; which thou hast wrought for them that trust in thee before the sons of men! Thou shalt hide them in the secret of thy presence from the pride of man: thou shalt keep them secretly in a pavilion from the strife of tongues.

Ps 31:19-20 KJ

FEELING OVERWHELMED

A bruised reed shall he not break, and the smoking flax shall he not quench: he shall bring forth judgment unto truth.

Isa 42:3 KJ

Tell the righteous it will be well with them, for they will enjoy the fruit of their deeds.

Isa 3:10 NIV

When thou passest through the waters, I will be with thee; and through the rivers, they shall not overflow thee: when thou walkest through the fire, thou shalt not be burned; neither shall the flame kindle upon thee.

Isa 43:2 KJ

Fearfulness and trembling are come upon me, and horror hath overwhelmed me. As for me, I will call upon God; and the Lord shall save me. Evening, and morning, and at noon, will I pray, and cry aloud: and he shall hear my voice. He hath delivered my soul in peace from the battle that was against me: for there were many with me.

Ps 55:5, 16-18 KJ

We were overwhelmed by sins, you forgave our transgressions. Blessed are those you choose and bring near to live in your courts! We are filled with the good things of your house, of your holy temple.

Ps 65:3-4 NIV

The Lord himself will fight for you. Just stay calm.

Ex 14:14 NLT

Many people say, "Who will show us better times?" Let your face smile on us, Lord. You have given me greater joy then those who have abundant harvests of grain and new wine.

Ps 4:6-7 NLT

He gives power to the weak and strength to the powerless. Even youths will become weak and tired, and young men will fall in exhaustion. But those who trust in the Lord will find new strength. They will soar high on wings like eagles. They will run and not grow weary. They will walk and not faint.

Isa 40:29-31 NLT

This I recall to my mind, therefore have I hope. It is of the Lord's mercies that we are not consumed, because his compassions fail not. They are new every morning: great is thy faithfulness.

Lam 3:21-23 KJ

FORGIVENESS

For if ye forgive men their trespasses, your heavenly Father will also forgive you: But if ye forgive not men their trespasses, neither will your Father forgive your trespasses.

Mt 6:14-15 KJ

This is my blood of the covenant, which is poured out for many for the forgiveness of sins.

Mt 26:28 NIV

And I will cleanse them from all their iniquity, whereby they have sinned against me; and I will pardon all their iniquities,

Susan Eaves

whereby they have sinned, and whereby they have transgressed against me.

Jer 33:8 KJ

He hath not dealt with us after our sins; nor rewarded us according to our iniquities. For as the heaven is high above the earth, so great is his mercy toward them that fear him. As far as the east is from the west, so far hath he removed our transgressions from us.

Ps 103:10-12 KJ

Peace I leave with you, my peace I give unto you: not as the world giveth, give I unto you. Let not your heart be troubled, neither let it be afraid.

Jn 14:27 KJ

And I will cleanse them from all the guilt and iniquity by which they have sinned against Me, and I will forgive all their guilt and iniquities by which they have sinned and rebelled against Me.

Jer 33:8 AMP

GOD'S FAITHFULNESS

Understand, therefore, that the Lord your God is indeed God. He is the faithful God who keeps his covenant for a thousand generations and lavishes his unfailing love on those who love him and obey his commands.

Deut 7:9 NLT

He is the Rock, his works are perfect, and all his ways are just. A faithful God who does no wrong, upright and just is he.

Deut 32:4 NIV

There hath no temptation taken you but such as is common to man: but God is faithful, who will not suffer you to be tempted above that ye are able; but will with the temptation also make a way to escape, that ye may be able to bear it.

1 Cor 10:13 KJ

For the word of the Lord is right and true; he is faithful in all he does.

Ps 33:4 NIV

To the faithful you show yourself faithful, to the blameless you show yourself blameless.

2 Sam 22:26 NIV

For the mountains shall depart, and the hills be removed; but my kindness shall not depart from thee, neither shall the covenant of my peace be removed, saith the Lord that hath mercy on thee.

Isa 54:10 KJ

He that spared not his own Son, but delivered him up for us all, how shall he not with him also freely give us all things?

Rom 8:32 KJ

I will instruct thee and teach thee in the way which thou shall go: I will guide thee with mine eye.

Ps 32:8 KJ

If ye abide in me, and my words abide in you, ye shall ask what
ye will, and it shall be done unto you.

Jn 15:7 KJ

GOD'S FORGIVENESS

Blessed is he whose transgressions are forgiven, whose sins are
covered. Blessed is the man whose sin the Lord does not count
against him and in whose spirit is no deceit. When I kept
silent, my bones wasted away through my groaning all day
long. For day and night your hand was heavy upon me; my
strength was sapped as in the heat of summer. Selah Then I
acknowledged my sin to you and did not cover up my iniquity. I said, "I will confess my transgressions to the Lord" - and
you forgave the guilt of my sin. Selah

Ps 32:1-5 NIV

For I will be merciful to their unrighteousness, and their sins
and their iniquities will I remember no more.

Heb 8:12 KJ

He hath not dealt with us after our sins; nor rewarded us
according to our iniquities. For as the heaven is high above
the earth, so great is his mercy toward them that fear him. As
far as the east is from the west, so far hath he removed our
transgressions from us.

Ps 103:10-12 KJ

If we confess our sins, he is faithful and just to forgive us our sins, and to cleanse us from all unrighteousness.

1 Jn 1:9 KJ

"I tell you, her sins - and they are many - have been forgiven, so she has shown me much love. But a person who is forgiven little shows only little love."

Lk 7:47 NLT

GOD'S PLANS FOR YOU

For I know the plans I have for you, declares the Lord, plans to prosper you and not to harm you, plans to give you hope and a future.

Jer 29:11 NIV

To give light to them that sit in darkness and in the shadow of death, to guide our feet into the way of peace.

Lk 1:79 KJ

That he would grant unto us, that we being delivered out of the hand of our enemies might serve him without fear, In holiness and righteousness before him, all the days of our life.

Lk 1:74-75 KJ

I beseech you therefore, brethren, by the mercies of God, that ye present your bodies a living sacrifice, holy, acceptable unto God, which is your reasonable service. And be not conformed to this world: but be ye transformed by the renewing of your mind, that ye may prove what is that good, and acceptable, and perfect, will of God.

Rom 12:1-2 KJ

The God of my rock; in him will I trust: he is my shield, and the horn of my salvation, my high tower, and my refuge, my saviour; thou savest me from violence.

2 Sa 22:3 KJ

Trust in the Lord with all your heart; do not depend on your own understanding. Seek his will in all you do, and he will show you which path to take.

Pr 3:5-6 NLT

Remember the things I have done in the past. For I alone am God! I am God, and there is none like me.

Isa 46:9 NLT

But whoso hearkens to me [Wisdom] shall dwell securely and in confident trust and shall be quiet, without fear or dread of evil.

Pr 1:33 AMP

Ye have not chosen me, but I have chosen you, and ordained you, that ye should go and bring forth fruit, and that your fruit should remain: that whatsoever ye shall ask of the Father in my name, he may give it you.

Jn 15:16 KJ

And the Lord shall deliver me from every evil work, and will preserve me unto his heavenly kingdom: to whom be glory for ever and ever. Amen.

2 Tim 4:18 KJ

The way of the Lord is strength to the upright: but destruction shall be to the workers of iniquity.

Pr 10:29 KJ

GOD'S POWER

"Be strong and courageous, Do not be afraid or discouraged because of the king of Assyria and the vast army with him, for there is a greater power with us than with him. With him is only the arm of flesh, but with us is the Lord our God to help us and to fight our battles."

2 Chr 32:7-8 NIV

The people that do know their God shall be strong and do exploits.

Dan 11:32 KJ

For he that is mighty hath done to me great things; and holy is his name. He hath shewed strength with his arm; he hath scattered the proud in the imagination of their hearts.

Lk 1:49, 51 KJ

His wisdom is profound, his power is vast. Who has resisted him and come out unscathed? He moves mountains without their knowing it and overturns them in his anger.

Job 9:4-5 NIV

You, who bring good tiding to Zion, go up on a high mountain. You, who bring good tidings to Jerusalem, lift up your voice with a shout, lift it up, do not be afraid; say to the towns of Judah, "Here is your God!" See, the Sovereign Lord comes with power, and his arm rules for him. See, his reward is with him, and his recompense accompanies him.

Isa 40:9-10 NIV

Now unto him that is able to do exceeding abundantly above all that we ask or think, according the power that worketh in us.

Eph 3:20 KJ

And what is the exceeding greatness of his power to us-ward who believe, according to the working of his mighty power, Which he wrought in Christ, when he raised him from the dead, and set him at his own right hand in the heavenly places, Far above all principality, and power, and might and dominion, and every name that is named not only in this world, but also in that which is to come.

Eph 1:19-21 KJ

But ye shall receive power, after that the Holy Ghost is come upon you.

Acts 1:8 KJ

GOD'S UNCONDITIONAL LOVE

For the Father himself loveth you, because ye have loved me, and have believed that I came out from God.

Jn 16:27 KJ

Let your conversation be without covetousness; and be content with such things as ye have: for he hath said, I will never leave thee, nor forsake thee.

Heb 13:5 KJ

In this was manifested the love of God toward us, because that God sent his only begotten Son into the world, that we might live through him. Herein is love, not that we loved God, but that he loved us, and sent his Son to be the propitiation for our sins.

1 Jn 4:9-10 KJ

For God so loved the world, that he gave his only begotten Son, that whosoever believeth in him should not perish, but have everlasting life.

Jn 3:16 KJ

Call unto me, and I will answer thee, and show thee great and mighty things, which thou knowest not.

Jer 33:3 KJ

But because the Lord loved you, and because he would keep the oath which he had sworn unto your fathers, hath the Lord brought you out with a mighty hand, and redeemed you out of the house of bondmen, from the hand of Pharaoh king of Egypt.

Deut 7:8 KJ

The Lord thy God in the midst of thee is mighty; he will save, he will rejoice over thee with joy; he will rest in his love, he will joy over thee with singing.

Zeph 3:17 KJ

Yet the Lord will command his loving kindness in the day time, and in the night his song shall be with me, and my prayer unto the God of my life.

Ps 42:8 KJ

But God commendeth his love toward us, in that, while we were yet sinners, Christ died for us.

Rom 5:8 KJ

GUIDANCE

In your unfailing love you will lead the people you have redeemed. In your strength you will guide them to your holy dwelling.

Ex 15:13 NIV

Show me your ways, O Lord, teach me your paths; guide me in your truth and teach me, for you are God my Savior, and my hope is in you all day long.

Ps 25:4-5 NIV

I have taught thee in the way of wisdom; I have led thee in right paths.

Pr 4:11 KJ

When thou goest, it shall lead thee; when thou sleepest, it shall keep thee; and when thou awakest, it shall talk with thee. For the commandment is a lamp; and the law is light; and reproofs of instruction are the way of life.

Pr 6:22-23 KJ

Guide my steps by your word, so I will not be overcome with evil.

Ps 119:133 NLT

Honesty guides good people.

Pr 11:3 NLT

Trust in the Lord with all your heart; do not depend on your own understanding. Seek his will in all you do, and he will show you what path to take.

Pr 3:5-6 NLT

Thy word is a lamp unto my feet and a light unto my path.

Ps 119:105 KJ

A man's heart diviseth his way: but the Lord directeth his steps.

Pr 16:9 KJ

For ye shall go out with joy, and be led forth with peace: the mountains and the hills shall break forth before you into singing, and all the trees of the field shall clap their hands.

Isa 55:12 KJ

HAIR LOSS

But there shall not a hair of your head perish.

Lk 21:18 KJ

But if a woman has long hair, it is a glory to her: for her hair is given her for a covering.

1 Cor 11:15 KJ

But even the very hairs of your head are all numbered. Fear not therefore: ye are of more value than many sparrows.

Lk 12:7 KJ

Wherefore I pray you to take some meat: for this is for your health: for there shall not a hair fall from the head of any of you.

Acts 27:34 KJ

In this passage Paul was talking about ruthless Roman soldiers and hard core criminals, if God would do this for them, how much more his own children?

HIDDEN THINGS

The secret of the Lord is with them that fear him, and he will shew them his covenant.

Ps 25:14 KJ

He revealeth the deep and secret things: he knoweth what is in the darkness, and the light dwelleth with him.

Dan 2:22 KJ

And it was revealed unto him by the Holy Ghost, that he should not see death, before he had seen the Lord's Christ.

Lk 2:26 KJ

But there is a God in heaven that revealeth secrets.

Dan 2:28 KJ

Surely the Lord God will do nothing, but he revealeth his secret unto his servants the prophets.

Amos 3:7 KJ

The secret things belong unto the Lord our God: but those things which are revealed belong unto us and to our children for ever, that we may do all the words of this law.

Deut 29:29 KJ

Having made known unto us the mystery of his will, according to his good pleasure which he hath purposed in himself.

Eph 1:9 KJ

Then was the secret revealed unto Daniel in a night vision. Then Daniel blessed the God of heaven.

Dan 2:19 KJ

Delight thyself also in the Lord: and he shall give thee the desires of thine heart.

Ps 37:4 KJ

HINDERANCES

Son of man, what is that proverb that ye have in the land of Israel, saying, The days are prolonged, and every vision faileth? Tell the people, 'This is what the Sovereign Lord says: I will put an end to this proverb, and you will soon stop quoting it.'

Now give them this new proverb to replace the old one: 'The time has come for every prophecy to be fulfilled!'

Ezek 12:22-23 NLT

This vision is for a future time. It describes the end, and it will be fulfilled. If it seems slow in coming, wait patiently, for it will surely take place. It will not be delayed.

Hab 2:3 NLT

If my people, which are called by my name, shall humble themselves, and pray, and seek my face, and turn from their wicked ways; then will I hear from heaven, and will forgive their sin, and will heal their land.

2 Chr 7:14 KJ

That by two immutable things, in which it was impossible for God to lie, we might have a strong consolation, who have fled for refuge to lay hold upon the hope set before us: Which hope we have as an anchor of the soul, both sure and stedfast, and which entereth into that within the veil.

Heb 6:18-19 KJ

For the vision is yet for an appointed time, but at the end it shall speak, and not lie: though it tarry wait for it: because it will surely come, it will not tarry.

Hab 2:3 KJ

Fear not, Daniel: for from the first day that thou didst set thine heart to understand and to chasten thyself before thy God, thy words were heard, and I am come for thy words.

Dan 10:12 KJ

Oh, that my people would listen to me! Oh, that Israel would follow me, walking in my paths! How quickly I would then subdue their enemies! How soon my hands would be upon their foes!

Ps 81:13-14 NLT

HUMILIATION

Instead of shame and dishonor, you will enjoy a double share of honor. You will possess a double portion of prosperity in your land, and everlasting joy will be yours.

Isa 61:7 NLT

Those who look to him for help will be radiant with joy; no shadow of shame will darken their faces.

Ps 34:5 NLT

Your promise revives me; it comforts me in all my troubles.

Ps 119:50 NLT

To rescue us from the hand of our enemies, and to enable us to serve him without fear

Lk 1:74 NIV

For God hath not given us the spirit of fear; but of power, and of love, and of a sound mind.

2 Tim 1:7 KJ

I weep with sorrow; encourage me by your word.

Ps 119:28 NLT

But this I recall and therefore have I hope and expectation: It is because of the Lord's mercy and loving-kindness that we are not consumed, because His [tender] compassions fail not. They are new every morning: great and abundant is Your stability and faithfulness. The Lord is my portion or share, says my living being (my inner self): therefore will I hope in Him and wait expectantly for Him.

Lam 3:21-24 AMP

INSANITY

Those who know your name trust in you, for you, O Lord, do not abandon those who search for you.

Ps 9:10 NLT

Turn my eyes from worthless things, and give me life through your word.

Ps 119:37 NLT

O Lord, listen to my cry; give me the discerning mind you promised.

Ps 119:169 NLT

The mind of sinful man is death, but the mind controlled by the Spirit is life and peace.

Ro 8:6 NIV

Finally, brothers, whatever is true, whatever is noble, whatever is right, whatever is pure, whatever is lovely, whatever is admirable—if anything is excellent or praiseworthy—think about such things.

Phil 4:8 NIV

Thou wilt keep him in perfect peace, whose mind is stayed on thee: because he trusteth in thee.

Isa 26:3 KJ

Therefore, since we have been justified through faith, we have peace with God through our Lord Jesus Christ.

Ro 5:1 NIV

O Lord, you took up my case; you redeemed my life.

Lam 3:25 NIV

Lean on, trust in, and be confident in the Lord with all your heart and mind and do not rely on your own insight or understanding. In all your ways know, recognize and acknowledge Him, and He will direct and make straight and plain your paths. It shall be health to your nerves and sinews, and marrow and moistening to your bones.

Pr 3:5-6, 8 AMP

For as he thinketh in his heart, so is he.

Pr 23:7 KJ

And be not conformed to this world: but be ye transformed by the renewing of your mind, that ye may prove what is that good, and acceptable, and perfect, will of God.

Rom 12:2 KJ

INSUFFICIENT FUNDS

If you will only obey me, you will have plenty to eat.

Isa 1:19 NLT

In all that he did in the service of the Temple of God and in his efforts to follow God's laws and commands, Hezekiah sought his God wholeheartedly. As a result, he was very successful.

2 Chr 31:21 NLT

Then answered I them, and said unto them, The God of heaven, he will prosper us; therefore we his servants will arise and build.

Neh 2:20 KJ

Now, my son, the Lord be with you, and may you have success and build the house of the Lord your God, as he said you would. May the Lord give you discretion and understanding when he puts you in command over Israel, so that you may keep the law of the Lord your God. Then you will have success if you are careful to observe the decrees and laws that the Lord gave Moses for Israel. Be strong and courageous. Do not be afraid or discouraged.

1 Chr 22:11-13 NIV

Bring ye all the tithes into the storehouse, that there may be meat in mine house, and prove me now herewith, saith the Lord of hosts, if I will not open you the windows of heaven, and pour you out a blessing, that there shall not be room enough to receive it.

Mal 3:10 KJ

But my God shall supply all your need according to his riches in glory by Christ Jesus.

Phil 4:19 KJ

And ye shall eat in plenty, and be satisfied, and praise the name of the Lord your God that hath dealt wondrously with you: and my people shall never be ashamed.

Joel 2:26 KJ

Praise ye the Lord. Blessed is the man that feareth the Lord that delighteth greatly in his commandments. Wealth and riches shall be in his house.

Ps 112:1, 3 KJ

JEALOUSY

Do not envy a violent man or choose any of his ways, for the Lord detests a perverse man but takes the upright into his confidence.

Pr 3:31-32 KJ

Wrath is cruel, and anger is outrageous; but who is able to stand before envy? Faithful are the wounds of a friend; but the kisses of an enemy are deceitful.

Pr 27:4, 6 KJ

Set me as a seal upon thine heart, as a seal upon thine arm: for love is strong as death; jealousy is cruel as the grave: the coals thereof are coals of fire, which hath a most vehement flame.

SS 8:6 KJ

A heart at peace gives life to the body, but envy rots the bones.

Pr 14:30 NIV

Let us behave decently, as in the daytime, not in orgies and drunkenness, not in sexual immorality and debauchery, not in dissension and jealousy. Rather, clothe yourselves with the Lord Jesus Christ, and do not think about how to gratify the desires of the sinful nature.

Rom 13:13-14 NIV

Idolatry and witchcraft; hatred, discord, jealousy, fits of rage, selfish ambition, dissensions, factions and envy; drunkenness, orgies, and the like. I warn you, as I did before, that those who live like this will not inherit the kingdom of God.

Gal 5:20-21 NIV

Resentment kills a fool, and envy slay the simple. I myself have seen a fool taking root, but suddenly his house was cursed.

Job 5:2-3 NIV

JOB LOSS

Be strong and courageous. Do not be afraid or terrified because of them, for the Lord your God goes with you; he will never leave you nor forsake you.

Deut 31:6 NIV

Blessed be God, even the Father of our Lord Jesus Christ, the Father of mercies, and the God of all comfort; Who comforteth us in all our tribulation, that we may be able to comfort them which are in any trouble, by the comfort wherewith we ourselves are comforted of God.

2 Cor 1:3-4 KJ

I am with you always, even unto the end of the world. Amen.

Mt 28:20 KJ

Thus saith the Lord, thy Redeemer, the Holy One of Israel; I am the Lord thy God which teacheth thee to profit, which leadeth thee by the way that thou shouldest go.

Isa 48:17 KJ

Nevertheless I am continually with thee.

Ps 73:23 KJ

And, behold, I am with thee, and will keep thee in all places whither thou goest, and will bring thee again into this land; for I will not leave thee, until I have done that which I have spoken to thee of.

Ge 28:15 KJ

Fear not, little flock; for it is your Father's good pleasure to give you the kingdom.

Lk 12:32 KJ

Therefore take no thought saying, What shall we eat? or, What shall we drink? or, Wherewithal shall we be clothed? (For after all these things do the Gentile seek:) for your heavenly Father knoweth that ye have need of all these things. But seek ye first the kingdom, of God, and his righteousness; and all these things shall be added unto you.

Mt 6:31-33 KJ

I called upon the Lord in distress: the Lord answered me, and set me in a large place.

Ps 118:5 KJ

For surely there is an end; and thine expectation shall not be cut off.

Pr 23:18 KJ

The young lions do lack, and suffer hunger: but they that seek the Lord shall not want any good thing.

Ps 34:10 KJ

LEGAL

Lord, you are my lawyer! Plead my case! For you have redeemed my life. You have seen the wrong they have done to me, Lord. Be my judge, and prove me right.

Lam 3:58 NLT

You only need to remain calm; the Lord will fight for you.

Ex 14:14 NCV

The eternal God is thy refuge, and underneath are the everlasting arms: and he shall thrust out the enemy from before thee; and shall say, destroy them.

Deut 33:27 KJ

I will build you using fairness. You will be safe from those who would hurt you, so you will have nothing to fear. Nothing will come to make you afraid. I will not send anyone to attack you, and you will defeat those who do attack you. So no weapon that is used against you will defeat you. You will show that those who speak against you are wrong. These are the good things my servants receive. Their victory comes from me, says the Lord.

Isa 54:14-15, 17 NCV

How great is your goodness that you have stored up for those who fear you that you have given to those who trust you. You do this for all to see. You protect them by your presence from what people plan against them. You shelter them from evil words.

Ps 31:19-20 NCV

But let all those that put their trust in thee rejoice: let them ever shout for joy, because thou defendest them: let them also that love thy name be joyful in thee. For thou, Lord, wilt bless the righteous; with favour wilt thou compass him as with a shield.

Ps 5:11-12 KJ

Nevertheless the Lord thy God would not hearken unto Balaam; but the Lord thy God turned the curse into a blessing unto thee, because the Lord thy God loved thee.

Deu 23:4-5 KJ

For thou, Lord wilt bless the righteous; with favor wilt thou compass him as with a shield.

Ps 5:12 KJ

LONELINESS

And therefore will the Lord wait, that he may be gracious unto you, and therefore will he be exalted, that he may have mercy upon you: for the Lord is a God of judgment: blessed are all they that wait for him.

Isa 30:18 KJ

Keep your lives free from the love of money and be content with what you have, because God has said, "Never will I leave you; never will I forsake you."

Heb 13:5 NIV

When my father and my mother forsake me, then the Lord will take me up.

Ps 27:10 KJ

I will not leave you comfortless: I will come to you.

Jn 14:18 KJ

A father of the fatherless, and a judge of the widows, is God in his holy habitation. God setteth the solitary in families: he bringeth out those which are bound with chains: but the rebellious dwell in a dry land.

Ps 68:5-6 KJ

Teaching them to observe all things whatsoever I have commanded you: and, lo, I am with you always, even unto the end of the world.

Mt 28:20 KJ

Let your conversation be without covetousness; and be content with such things as ye have: for he hath said, I will never leave thee, nor forsake thee.

Heb 13:5 KJ

The eternal God is thy refuge, and underneath are the everlasting arms.

Deut 33:27 KJ

Henceforth I call you not servants; for the servant knoweth not what his Lord doeth: but I have called you friends; for all things that I have heard of my Father I have made known unto you.

Jn 15:15 KJ

MENTAL WARFARE

For this cause we also, since the day we heard it, do not cease to pray for you, and to desire that ye might be filled with the knowledge of his will in all wisdom and spiritual understanding; That ye might walk worthy of the Lord unto all pleasing, being fruitful in every good work, and increasing in the knowledge of God.

Col 1:9-10 KJ

The entrance of thy words giveth light; it giveth understanding unto the simple.

Ps 119:130 KJ

The Lord also will be a refuge for the oppressed, a refuge in times of trouble.

Ps 9:9 KJ

And let us not be weary in well doing: for in due season we shall reap, if we faint not.

Gal 6:9 KJ

Because the Sovereign Lord helps me, I will not be disgraced. Therefore, I have set my face like a stone, determined to do his will. And I know that I will not be put to shame.

Isa 50:7 NLT

And be not conformed to this world: but be ye transformed by the renewing of your mind, that ye may prove what is that good, and acceptable, and perfect, will of God.

Rom 12:2 KJ

For though we walk in the flesh, we do not war after the flesh: (For the weapons of our warfare are not carnal, but mighty through God to the pulling down of strong holds;) Casting down imaginations and every high thing that exalteth itself against the knowledge of God, and bringing into captivity every thought to the obedience of Christ;

2 Cor 10:3-5 KJ

MISTAKES

The Lord directs the steps of the godly. He delights in every detail of their lives. Though they stumble, they will never fall, for the Lord holds them by the hand.

Ps 37:23-24 NLT

For I am about to do something new. See, I have already begun! Do you not see it? I will make a pathway through the wilderness. I will create rivers in the dry wasteland.

Isa 43:19 NLT

Although the fig tree shall not blossom, neither shall fruit be in the vines; the labour of the olive shall fail, and the fields shall yield no meat; the flock shall be cut off from the fold, and there shall be no herd in the stalls: Yet I will rejoice in the Lord, I will joy in the God of my salvation.

Hab 3:17-18 KJ

Thou wilt not leave my soul in hell, neither wilt thou suffer thine Holy One to see corruption. Thou hast made known to me the ways of life: thou shalt make me full of joy with thy countenance.

Acts 2:27-28 KJ

Don't tear your clothing in your grief, but tear your hearts instead. Return to the Lord your God, for he is merciful and compassionate, slow to get angry and filled with unfailing love. He is eager to relent and not punish. Who knows? Perhaps he will give you a reprieve, sending you a blessing instead of this curse.

Joel 2:13 NLT

For if you live by its dictates, you will die. But if through the power of the Spirit you put to death the deeds of your sinful nature, you will live.

Rom 8:13 NLT

MOCKERS

Rejoice not against me, O mine enemy: when I fall, I shall arise; when I sit in darkness, the Lord shall be a light unto me.

Mic 7:8 KJ

They will fight you, but they will fail. For I am with you, and I will take care of you. I, the Lord, have spoken!

Jer 1:19 NLT

This is how the Lord responds: "If you return to me, I will restore you so you can continue to serve me. If you speak good words rather than worthless ones, you will be my spokesman. You must influence them; do not let them influence you! They will fight against you like an attacking army, but I will make you as secure as a fortified wall of bronze. They will not conquer you, for I am with you to protect and rescue you. I, the Lord, have spoken!"

Jer 15:19-20 NLT

O my God, I trust in thee: let me not be ashamed, let not mine enemies triumph over me. Yea, let none that wait on thee be ashamed: let them be ashamed which transgress without cause.

Ps 25:2-3 KJ

Cast not away therefore your confidence, which hath great recompence of reward.

Heb 10:35 KJ

Oh, that my people would listen to me! Oh, that Israel would follow me, walking in my paths! How quickly I would then subdue their enemies! How soon my hands would be upon their foes!

Ps 81:13-14 NLT

People who accept discipline are on the pathway to life, but those who ignore correction will go astray. Hiding hatred makes you a liar: slandering others makes you a fool.

Pr 10:17-18 NLT

God blesses you when people mock you and persecute you and lie about you and say all sorts of evil things against you because you are my followers. Be happy about it! Be very glad! For a great reward awaits you in heaven.

Mt 5:11-12 NLT

NEGATIVE EMOTIONS

In the multitude of my thoughts within me thy comforts delight my soul.

Ps 94:19 KJ

And whatsoever ye do in word or deed, do all in the name of the Lord Jesus, giving thanks to God and the Father by him.

Col 3:17 KJ

Let all that I am praise the Lord; may I never forget the good things he does for me.

Ps 103:2 NLT

Finally, brethren, whatsoever things are true, whatsoever things are honest, whatsoever things are just, whatsoever things are pure, whatsoever things are lovely, whatsoever things are of good report; if there be any virtue, and if there be any praise, think on these things.

Phil 4:8 KJ

I complained and my spirit was overwhelmed.

Ps 77:3 KJ

Beloved, I wish above all things that thou mayest prosper and be in health, even as thy soul prospereth.

3 Jn 1:2 KJ

I waited patiently for the Lord; and he inclined unto me, and heard my cry. He brought me up also out of an horrible pit, out of the miry clay, and set my feet upon a rock, and established my goings. And he hath put a new song in my mouth, even praise unto our God: many shall see it, and fear, and shall trust in the Lord. Blessed is that man that maketh the Lord his trust, and respecteth not the proud, nor such as turn aside to lies.

Ps 40: 1-4 KJ

He restoreth my soul: he leadeth me in the paths of righteousness for his name's sake.

Ps 23:3 KJ

NEGATIVE THOUGHTS

Rejoice in the Lord always: and again I say, Rejoice. Let your moderation be known unto all men. The Lord is at hand. Be careful for nothing; but in every thing by prayer and supplication with thanksgiving let your requests be made known unto God. And the peace of God, which passeth all understanding, shall keep your hearts and minds through Christ Jesus.

Phil 4:4-7 KJ

I cried out, "I am slipping!" but your unfailing love, O Lord, supported me. When doubts filled my mind, your comfort gave me renewed hope and cheer.

Ps 94:18-19 NLT

I will walk in freedom, for I have devoted myself to your commandments.

Ps 119:45 NLT

For from within, out of a person's heart, come evil thoughts, sexual immorality, theft, murder, adultery, greed, wickedness, deceit, lustful desires, envy, slander, pride, and foolishness. All these vile things come from within; they are what defile you.

Mk 7:21-23 NLT

Yea, let none that wait on thee be ashamed: let them be ashamed which transgress without cause.

Ps 25:3 KJ

Susan Eaves

Beloved, I wish above all things that thou mayest prosper and be in health, even as thy soul prospereth.

3Jn 1:2 KJ

OPPRESSION

The Lord is a shelter for the oppressed, a refuge in times of trouble.

Ps 9:9 NLT

You came near when I called you, and you said, "Do not fear." O Lord, you took up my case; you redeemed my life. You have seen, O Lord, the wrong done to me. Uphold my cause! You have seen the depth of their vengeance, all their plots against me.

Lam 3:58-60 NIV

"Pay attention, O Jacob, for you are my servant, O Israel. I, the Lord, made you, and I will not forget you. I have swept away your sins like a cloud. I have scattered your offenses like the morning mist. Oh, return to me, for I have paid the price to set you free."

Isa 44:21-22 NLT

Teach me, O Lord, the way of thy statutes; and I shall keep it unto the end.

Ps 119:33 KJ

How God anointed Jesus of Nazareth with the Holy Ghost and with power: who went about doing good, and healing all that were oppressed of the devil; for God was with him.

Acts 10:38 KJ

The Lord taketh my part with them that help me: therefore shall I see my desire upon them that hate me.

Ps 118:7 KJ

For they being ignorant of God's righteousness, and going about to establish their own righteousness, have not submitted themselves unto the righteousness of God. For Christ is the end of the law for righteousness to every one that believeth.

Rom 10:3-4 KJ

Those who cling to worthless idols forfeit the grace that could be theirs.

Jon 2:8 NIV

How God anointed Jesus of Nazareth with the Holy Spirit and with power, who went about doing good and healing all who were oppressed by the devil, for God was with him.

Acts 10:38 NKJ

Jesus Christ the same yesterday, and today and forever.

Heb 13:8 KJ

Susan Eaves

OVERCOMING BITTERNESS

In my distress I prayed to the Lord, and the Lord answered me and set me free. The Lord is for me, so I will have no fear. What can mere people do to me? Yes, the Lord is for me; he will help me. I will look in triumph at those who hate me.

Ps 118:5-7 NLT

For I will be merciful to their unrighteousness, and their sins and their iniquities will I remember no more.

Heb 8:12 KJ

But I confess my sins; I am deeply sorry for what I have done.

Ps 38:18 NLT

But those who trust in the Lord will find new strength. They will soar high on wings like eagles. They will run and not grow weary. They will walk and not faint.

Isa 40:31 NLT

But now put away and rid yourselves [completely] of all these things; anger, rage bad feeling toward others, curses and slander, and foulmouthed abuse and shameful utterance from your lips!

Col 3:8 AMP

The people will declare, "The Lord is the source of all my righteousness and strength." And all who were angry with him will come to him and be ashamed.

Isa 45:24 NLT

Thou wilt not leave my soul in hell. Thou hast made known to me the ways of life; thou shalt make me full of joy with thy countenance.

Acts 2:27-28 KJ

The discretion of a man deferreth his anger; and it is his glory to pass over a transgression.

Pr 19:11 KJ

Do not be quick in spirit to be angry or vexed, for anger and vexation lodge in the bosom of fools.

Eccl 7:9 AMP

He lifted me out of the pit of despair, out of the mud and the mire. He set my feet on solid ground and steadied me as I walked along.

Ps 40:2-3 NLT

Brethren, I count not myself to have apprehended: but this one thing I do, forgetting those things which are behind, and reaching forth unto those things which are before, I press toward the mark for the prize of the high calling of God in Christ Jesus.

Phil 3:13-14 KJ

Wherefore seeing we also are compassed about with so great a cloud of witnesses, let us lay aside every weight, and the sin which doth so easily beset us, and let us run with patience the race that is set before us, Looking unto Jesus the author and finisher of our faith; who for the joy that was set before him endured the cross, despising the shame, and is set down at the right hand of the throne of God.

Heb 12:1-2 KJ

OVERCOMING IDOLS

Do what is good and run from evil so that you may live! Then the Lord God of Heaven's Armies will be your helper, just as you have claimed. Hate evil and love what is good; turn your courts into true halls of justice. Perhaps even yet the Lord God of Heaven's Armies will have mercy on the remnant of his people.

Amos 5:14-15 NLT

They have not known nor understood: for he hath shut their eyes, that they cannot see; and their hearts, that they cannot understand.

Isa 44:18 KJ

Then he takes what's left and makes his god: a carved idol! He falls down in front of it, worshiping and praying to it. "Rescue me!" he says. "You are my god!"

Isa 44:17 NLT

Those who cling to worthless idols forfeit the grace that could be theirs.

Jn 2:8 NIV

The sorrows of those will increase who run after other gods.

Ps 16:4 NIV

Their sorrows shall be multiplied that hasten after another god.

Ps 16:4 KJ

They that observe lying vanities forsake their own mercy.

Jonah 2:8 KJ

OVERCOMING PRIDE

But when his heart and mind were puffed up with arrogance, he was brought down from his royal throne and stripped of his glory.

Dan 5:20 NLT

Since God chose you to be the holy people he loves, you must clothe yourselves with tenderhearted mercy, kindness, humility, gentleness, and patience.

Col 3:12 NLT

But he gives us more grace. That is why Scripture says: "God opposes the proud but gives grace to the humble."

Ja 4:6-7 NIV

And when he was at the place, he said unto them, Pray that ye enter not into temptation.

Lk 22:40 KJ

Though the Lord be high, yet hath he respect unto the lowly: but the proud he knoweth afar off.

Ps 138:6 KJ

Susan Eaves

The fear of the Lord is to hate evil: pride, and arrogancy, and the evil way, and the froward mouth, do I hate.

Pr 8:13 KJ

Pride goeth before destruction, and a haughty spirit before a fall. Better it is to be of a humble spirit with the lowly, than to divide the spoil with the proud.

Pr 16:18-19 KJ

You save the humble, but your eyes are on the haughty to bring them low.

2 Sam 22:28 NIV

He guides the humble in what is right and teaches them his way.

Ps 25:9 NIV

The humble will see their God at work and be glad. Let all who seek God's help be encouraged.

Ps 69:32 NLT

OVERCOMING SIN

Do not harden your hearts as you did at Meribah, as you did that day at Massah in the desert, where your fathers tested and tried me, though they had seen what I did. For forty years I was angry with that generation; I said, "They are a people whose hearts go astray, and they have not known my ways." So I declared on oath in my anger, "They shall never enter my rest."

Ps 95:8-11 NIV

And if Christ be in you, the body is dead because of sin; but the Spirit is life because of righteousness. But if the Spirit of him that raised up Jesus from the dead dwell in you, he that raised up Christ from the dead shall also quicken your mortal bodies by his Spirit that dwelleth in you.

Ro 8:10-11 KJ

So humble yourselves before God. Resist the devil, and he will flee from you. Come close to God, and God will come close to you. Wash your hands, you sinners; purify your hearts, for your loyalty is divided between God and the world.

Ja 4:7-8 NLT

The Lord knoweth how to deliver the godly out of temptations, and to reserve the unjust unto the day of judgment to be punished:

2 Pe 2:9 KJ

Be not deceived: evil communications corrupt good manners. Awake to righteousness, and sin not; for some have not the knowledge of God: I speak this to your shame.

1 Co 15:33-34 KJ

They promise them freedom, while they themselves are slaves of depravity—for a man is a slave to whatever has mastered him.

2 Pe 2:19 NIV

OVERCOMING TEMPTATION

Like a city whose walls are broken down is a man who lacks self-control.

Pr 25:28 NIV

I said, "I will watch my ways and keep my tongue from sin; I will put a muzzle on my mouth as long as the wicked are in my presence."

Ps 39:1 NIV

Afterward Jesus findeth him in the temple, and said unto him, Behold, thou art made whole: sin no more, lest a worse thing come unto thee.

Jn 5:14 KJ

Thy word have I hid in mine heart, that I might not sin against thee.

Ps 119:11 KJ

The Lord knoweth how to deliver the godly out of temptations, and to reserve the unjust unto the day of judgment to be punished:

2 Pet 2:9 KJ

For though we live in the world, we do not wage war as the world does. The weapons we fight with are not the weapons of the world. On the contrary, they have divine power to demolish strongholds. We demolish arguments and every pretension that sets itself up against the knowledge of God, and we take captive every thought to make it obedient to Christ.

2 Cor 10:3-5 NIV

What man is he that desireth life, and loveth many days, that he may see good? Keep thy tongue from evil and thy lips from speaking guile.

Ps 34:12 KJ

Or what shall a man give in exchange for his soul?

Mk 8:37 KJ

If thou doest well, shalt thou not be accepted? and if thou doest not well, sin lieth at the door.

Gen 4:7 KJ

OVERCOMING TORMENT

Lift up thine eyes round about, and behold: all these gather themselves together, and come to thee. As I live, saith the Lord, thou shalt surely clothe thee with them all, as with an ornament, and bind them on thee, as a bride doeth.

Isa 49:18 KJ

Casting all your care upon him; for he careth for you.

1 Pet 5:7 KJ

O Lord, I am your servant; yes, I am your servant, born into your household; you have freed me from my chains.

Ps 116:16 NLT

For by thy words thou shalt be justified, and by thy words thou shalt be condemned.

Mt 12:37 KJ

And, behold, two blind men sitting by the way side, when they heard that Jesus passed by, cried out, saying, Have mercy on us, O Lord, thou son of David.

Mt 20:30 KJ

In the day when I cried thou answeredst me, and strengthenedst me with strength in my soul.

Ps 138:3 KJ

Let not your heart be troubled: ye believe in God, believe also in me.

Jn 14:1 KJ

Being confident of this very thing, that he which hath begun a good work in you will perform it until the day of Jesus Christ:

Phil 1:6 KJ

The Lord your God which goeth before you, he shall fight for you, according to all that he did for you in Egypt before your eyes;

Deut 1:30 KJ

I will call upon the Lord, who is worthy to be praised: so shall I be saved from mine enemies.

Ps 18:3 KJ

Offer unto God thanksgiving; and pay thy vows unto the most High: And call upon me in the day of trouble: I will deliver thee, and thou shalt glorify me.

Ps 50:14-15 KJ

PAIN

He was despised and rejected - a man of sorrows, acquainted with deepest grief. We turned our backs on him and looked the other way. He was despised, and we did not care. Yet it was our weaknesses he carried; it was our sorrows that weighed him down. And we thought his troubles were a punishment from God, a punishment for his own sins! But he was pierced for our rebellion, crushed for our sins. He was beaten so we could be whole. He was whipped so we could be healed.

Isa 53:3-5 NLT

Feel my pain and see my trouble. Forgive all my sins.

Ps 25:18 NLT

And he said unto her, Daughter, thy faith hath made thee whole; go in peace, and be whole of thy plague.

Mk 5:34 KJ

He is chastened also with pain upon his bed, and the multitude of his bones with strong pain. Yea, his soul draweth near unto the grave, and his life to the destroyers. If there be a messenger with him, an interpreter, one among a thousand, to shew unto man his uprightness: Then he is gracious unto

him, and saith, Deliver him from going down to the pit: I
have found a ransom.

Job 33:19, 22-24 KJ

Jesus became your ransom.

Just as the Son of Man did not come to be served, but to serve,
and to give his life as a ransom for many.

Mt 20:28 NIV

Who forgiveth all thine iniquities; who healeth all thy diseases.

Ps 103:3 KJ

He personally carried our sins in his body on the cross so that
we can be dead to sin and live for what is right. By his wounds
you are healed.

1 Pe 2:24 NLT

Let us therefore come boldly unto the throne of grace, that
we may obtain mercy, and find grace to help in time of need.

Heb 4:16 KJ

PAINFUL MEMORIES

Blessed be God, even the Father of our Lord Jesus Christ, the
Father of mercies, and the God of all comfort. Who comforteth us in all our tribulation, that we may be able to comfort
them which are in any trouble, by the comfort wherewith we
ourselves are comforted of God.

2 Cor 1:3-4 KJ

If only you would prepare your heart and lift up your hands to him in prayer! You will forget your misery; it will be like water flowing away. Your life will be brighter than the noonday. Even darkness will be as bright as morning. Having hope will give you courage. You will be protected and will rest in safety.

Job 11:13, 16-18 NLT

For since the beginning of the world men have not heard, nor perceived by the ear, neither hath the eye seen, O God, beside thee, what he hath prepared for him that waiteth for him.

Isa 64:4 KJ

Brethren, I count not myself to have apprehended: but this one thing I do, forgetting those things which are behind, and reaching forth unto those things which are before, I press toward the mark for the prize of the high calling of God in Christ Jesus.

Phil 3:13-14 KJ

This is my comfort in my affliction: for thy word hath quickened me.

Ps 119:50 KJ

For the Lord shall comfort Zion: he will comfort all her waste places; and he will make her wilderness like Eden, and her desert like the garden of the Lord; joy and gladness shall be found therein, thanksgiving, and the voice of melody.

Isa 51:3 KJ

As one whom his mother comforteth, so will I comfort you; and ye shall be comforted in Jerusalem.

Isa 66:13 KJ

Look upon mine affliction and my pain; and forgive all my sins.

Ps 25:18 KJ

He heals the brokenhearted and bandages their wounds.

Ps 147:3 NLT

PEACE

For unto us a child is born, unto us a son is given: and the government shall be upon his shoulder: and his name shall be called Wonderful, Counselor, The mighty God, The everlasting Father, The Prince of Peace.

Isa 9:6 KJ

And, having made peace through the blood of his cross, by him to reconcile all things unto himself; by him, I say, whether they be things in earth, or things in heaven.

Col 1:20 KJ

And my people shall dwell in a peaceable habitation, and in sure dwellings, and in quiet resting places.

Isa 32:18 KJ

And not only so, but we also joy in God through our Lord Jesus Christ, by whom we have now received the atonement.

Ro 5:11 KJ

Be careful for nothing; but in every thing by prayer and supplication with thanksgiving let your requests be made known unto God. And the peace of God, which passeth all understanding, shall keep your hearts and minds through Christ Jesus.

Phil 4:6-7 KJ

Let the peace of Christ rule in your hearts, since as members of one body you were called to peace. And be thankful.

Col 3:15 NIV

Therefore being justified by faith, we have peace with God through our Lord Jesus Christ: By whom also we have access by faith into this grace wherein we stand, and rejoice in hope of the glory of God.

Rom 5:1-2 KJ

These things I have spoken unto you, that in me ye might have peace. In the world ye shall have tribulation: but be of good cheer; I have overcome the world.

Jn 16:33 KJ

PROBLEM SOLVING

The fear of the Lord is the beginning of wisdom; all who follow his precepts have good understanding.

Ps 111:10 NIV

Guide my steps by your word, so I will not be overcome by evil.

Ps 119:133 NLT

And this is the confidence that we have in him that, if we ask any thing according to his will, he heareth us: And if we know that he hear us, whatsoever we ask, we know that we have the petitions that we desired of him.

1 Jn 5:14-15 KJ

This poor man cried, and the Lord heard him, and saved him out of all his troubles.

Ps 34:6 KJ

Let not mercy and truth forsake thee: bind them about thy neck; write them upon the table of thine heart: So shalt thou find favour and good understanding in the sight of God and man.

Pr 3:3-4 KJ

Hear instruction, and be wise, and refuse it not. Blessed is the man that heareth me, watching daily at my gates, waiting at the posts of my doors. For whoso findeth me findeth life, and shall obtain favour of the Lord.

Pr 8:33-35 KJ

In my distress I prayed to the Lord, and the Lord answered me and set me free. The Lord is for me, so I will have no fear. What can mere people do to me? Yes, the Lord is for me; he will help me. I will look in triumph at those who hate me.

Ps 118:5-7 NLT

In every thing give thanks: for this is the will of God in Christ Jesus concerning you.

1 Thess 5:18 KJ

And thine ears shall hear a word behind thee, saying, This is the way, walk ye in it, when ye turn to the right hand, and when ye turn to the left.

Isa 30:21 KJ

PROTECTION

O Lord, I have come to you for protection; don't let me be disgraced. Save me, for you do what is right. Turn your ear to listen to me; rescue me quickly. Be my rock of protection, a fortress where I will be safe. You are my rock and my fortress. For the honor of your name, lead me out of this danger. Pull me from the trap my enemies set for me, for I find protection in you alone.

Ps 31:1-4 NLT

He that dwelleth in the secret place of the most High shall abide under the shadow of the Almighty. I will say of the Lord, He is my refuge and my fortress: my God; in him will I trust. Surely he shall deliver thee from the snare of the fowler, and from the noisome pestilence.

Ps 91:1-3 KJ

Thou shalt not be afraid for the terror by night; nor for the arrow that flieth by day; Nor for the pestilence that walketh in darkness; nor for the destruction that wasteth at noonday.

Ps 91:5-6 KJ

For he shall give his angels charge over thee, to keep thee in all thy ways.

Ps 91:11 KJ

Susan Eaves

Because he hath set his love upon me, therefore will I deliver him: I will set him on high, because he hath known my name. He shall call upon me, and I will answer him: I will be with him in trouble; I will deliver him, and honour him.

Ps 91:14-15 KJ

And I will make with them a covenant of peace, and will cause the evil beasts to cease out of the land: and they shall dwell safely in the wilderness, and sleep in the woods.

Ezek 34:25 KJ

The eternal God is thy refuge, and underneath are the everlasting arms: and he shall thrust out the enemy from before thee; and shall say, Destroy them.

Deut 33:27 KJ

PURPOSE

Call unto me, and I will answer thee, and show thee great and mighty things, which thou knowest not.

Jer 33:3 KJ

"I knew you before I formed you in your mother's womb. Before you were born I set you apart and appointed you as my prophet to the nations."

Jer 1:5 NLT

And the Lord answered me, and said, Write the vision, and make it plain upon tables, that he may run that readeth it.

Hab 2:2 KJ

Trust in the Lord with all thine heart; and lean not unto thine own understanding. In all thy ways acknowledge him, and he shall direct thy paths.

Pr 3:5-6 KJ

But as for you, ye thought evil against me; but God meant it unto good, to bring to pass, as it is this day, to save much people alive.

Gen 50:20 KJ

The entrance of thy words giveth light; it giveth understanding unto the simple.

Ps 119:130 KJ

Thou wilt shew me the path of life: in thy presence is fulness of joy; at thy right hand there are pleasures for evermore.

Ps 16:11 KJ

For this God is our God forever and ever: he will be our guide even unto death.

Ps 48:14 KJ

And we know that all things work together for good to them that love God, to them who are the called according to his purpose.

Rom 8:28 KJ

For we are his workmanship, created in Christ Jesus unto good works, which God hath before ordained that we should walk in them.

Eph 2:10 KJ

REJECTION

God does not reject a blameless man or strengthen the hands of evildoers. He will yet fill your mouth with laughter and your lips with shouts of joy.

Job 8:20-21 NIV

For I will restore health unto thee, and I will heal thee of thy wounds, saith the Lord; because they called thee an Outcast, saying, This is Zion, whom no man seeketh after.

Jer 30:17 KJ

God, who knows the heart, showed that he accepted them by giving the Holy Spirit to them, just as he did to us.

Acts 15:8 NIV

To the praise of the glory of his grace, wherein he hath made us accepted in the beloved.

Eph 1:6 KJ

But thou, O Lord, art a shield for me; my glory, and the lifter up of mine head.

Ps 3:3 KJ

When men are cast down, then thou shalt say, There is lifting up; and he shall save the humble person.

Job 22:29 KJ

Yet it was our weaknesses he carried; it was our sorrows that weighed him down. And we thought his troubles were a punishment from God, a punishment for his own sins! But he was pierced for our rebellion, crushed for our sins. He was beaten so we could be whole. He was whipped so we could be healed.

Isa 53:4-5 NLT

I will set My dwelling in and among you, and My soul shall not despise or reject or separate itself from you.

Lev 26:11 AMP

You did not choose me, but I chose you and appointed you to go and bear fruit - fruit that will last. Then the Father will give you whatever you ask in my name.

Jn 15:16 NIV

SECOND CHANCES

Then the Lord spoke to Jonah a second time: "Get up and go to the great city of Nineveh, and deliver the message I have given you."

Jn 3:1-2 NLT

I used to wander off until you disciplined me; but now I closely follow your word.

Ps 119:67 NLT

But he was pierced for our rebellion, crushed for our sins. He was beaten so we could be whole. He was whipped so we could be healed.

Isa 53:5 NLT

Jesus looked at them intently and said, "Humanly speaking, it is impossible. But not with God. Everything is possible with God."

Mk 10:27 NLT

Rend your heart and not your garments. Return to the Lord your God, for he is gracious and compassionate, slow to anger and abounding in love, and he relents from sending calamity. Who knows? He may turn and have pity and leave behind a blessing.

Joel 2:13-14 NIV

His mother saith unto the servants, Whatsoever he saith unto you, do it.

Jn 2:5 KJ

Why art thou cast down, O my soul? and why art thou disquieted within me? hope thou in God: for I shall yet praise him, who is the health of my countenance, and my God.

Ps 42:11 KJ

He looketh upon men, and if any say, I have sinned, and perverted that which was right, and it profited me not; He will deliver his soul from going into the pit, and his life shall see the light. Lo, all these things worketh God oftentimes with man.

Job 33:27-29 KJ

SECURITY

As for God, his way is perfect; the word of the Lord is tried: he is a buckler to all them that trust in him.

2 Sam 22:31 KJ

Trust in the Lord and do good. Then you will live safely in the land and prosper. Take delight in the Lord, and he will give you your heart's desires. Commit everything you do to the Lord. Trust him, and he will help you.

Ps 37:3-5 NLT

And it shall be said in that day, Lo, this is our God; we have waited for him, and he will save us; this is the Lord; we have waited for him, we will be glad and rejoice in his salvation.

Isa 25:9 KJ

They will live in prosperity, and their children will inherit the land.

Ps 25:13 NLT

Those who know your name will trust in you, for you, Lord, have never forsaken those who seek you.

Ps 9:10 NIV

But I trust in your unfailing love; my heart rejoices in your salvation.

Ps 13:5 NIV

May the God of hope fill you with all joy and peace as you trust in him, so that you may overflow with hope by the power of the Holy Spirit.

Rom 15:13 NIV

Why are thou cast down, O my soul? And why are thou disquieted in me? Hope thou in God: for I shall yet praise him for the help of his countenance.

Ps 42:5 KJ

Whither shall I go from thy spirit? Or whither shall I flee from they presence? If I ascend up into heaven, thou are there; if I make my bed in hell, behold, thou art there. Even there shall thy hand lead me, and thy right hand shall hold me.

Ps 139:7-8, 10 KJ

SELF HATRED

I will praise thee; for I am fearfully and wonderfully made: marvelous are thy works; and that my soul knoweth right well.

Ps 139:14 KJ

In conclusion, be strong in the Lord [be empowered through your union with Him]; draw your strength from Him [that strength which His boundless might provides].

Eph 6:10 AMP

Whereby are given unto us exceeding great and precious promises: that by these ye might be partakers of the divine nature, having escaped the corruption that is in the world through lust.

2 Pet 1:4 KJ

To the praise of the glory of his grace, wherein he hath made us accepted in the beloved.

Eph 1:6 KJ

For whom he did foreknow, he also did predestinate to be conformed to the image of his Son, that he might be the first-born among many brethren.

Rom 8:29 KJ

And this hope will not lead to disappointment. For we know how dearly God loves us, because he has given us the Holy Spirit to fill our hearts with his love.

Rom 5:5 NLT

SELF-DOUBT

Light shines in the darkness for the godly. They are generous, compassionate, and righteous.

Ps 112:4 NLT

There is therefore now no condemnation to them which are in Christ Jesus, who walk not after the flesh, but after the Spirit.

Rom 8:1 KJ

But of him are ye in Christ Jesus, who of God is made unto us wisdom, and righteousness, and sanctification, and redemption.

1 Co 1:30 KJ

Now thanks be unto God, which always causeth us to triumph in Christ, and maketh manifest the savour of his knowledge by us in every place.

2 Co 2:14 KJ

And ye are complete in him, which is the head of all principality and power.

Col 2:10 KJ

But let all who take refuge in you rejoice; let them sing joyful praises forever. Spread your protection over them, that all who love your name may be filled with joy. For you bless the godly, O Lord; you surround them with your shield of love.

Ps 5:11-12 NLT

The Lord did not set his heart on you and choose you because you were more numerous than other nations, for you were the smallest of all nations! Rather, it was simply that the Lord loves you.

Deut 8:7-8 NLT

In all thy ways acknowledge him, and he shall direct thy paths.

Pr 3:6 KJ

And let us not be weary in well doing: for in due season we shall reap, if we faint not.

Gal 6:9 KJ

SICKNESS

And said, If thou wilt diligently hearken to the voice of the Lord thy God, and wilt do that which is right in his sight, and wilt give ear to his commandments, and keep all his statutes, I will put none of these diseases upon thee, which I have brought upon the Egyptians: for I am the Lord that healeth thee.

Ex 15:26 KJ

He forgives all my sins and heals all my diseases.

Ps 103:3 NCV

O Lord my God, I cried unto thee, and thou hast healed me.

Ps 30:2 KJ

I will never forget your commandments, for by them you give me life.

Ps 119:93 NLT

But unto you that fear my name shall the Sun of righteousness arise with healing in his wings; and ye shall go forth, and grow up as calves of the stall.

Mal 4:2 KJ

Who his own self bare our sins in his own body on the tree that we, being dead to sins, should live unto righteousness: by whose stripes ye were healed.

1 Pet 2:24 KJ

Susan Eaves

By stretching forth thine hand to heal; and that signs and wonders may be done by the name of thy holy child Jesus.

Acts 4:30 KVJ

Then touched he their eyes, saying, According to your faith be it unto you.

Mt 9:29 KJ

He sent his word, and healed them, and delivered them from their destructions.

Ps 107:20 KJ

My child, pay attention to what I say, Listen carefully to my words, don't lose sight of them. Let them penetrate deep into your heart, for they bring life to those who find them, and healing to their whole body.

Pr 4:20-22 NLT

Some were fools; they rebelled and suffered for their sins. They couldn't stand the thought of food, and they were knocking on death's door. "Lord, help!" they cried in their trouble, and he saved them from their distress. He sent out his word and healed them, snatching them from the door of death.

Ps 107:17-20 NLT

If God did this for fools, how much more his own children?

SLANDER

Commit everything you do to the Lord. Trust him, and he will help you. He will make your innocence radiate like the dawn, and the justice of your cause will shine like the noonday sun.

Ps 37:5-6 NLT

Thus saith the Lord, thy redeemer, and he that formed thee from the womb, I am the Lord that maketh all things; that stretcheth forth the heavens alone; that spreadeth abroad the earth by myself; That frustrateth the tokens of the liars, and maketh diviners mad; that turneth wise men backward, and maketh their knowledge foolish; That confirmeth the word of his servant, and performeth the counsel of his messengers; that saith to Jerusalem, Thou shalt be inhabited; and to the cities of Judah, Ye shall be built, and I will raise up the decayed places there.

Isa 44:24-26 KJ

Give ear to my words, O Lord, consider my sighing. Listen to my cry for help, my King and my God, for to you I pray. In the morning, O Lord, you hear my voice; in the morning I lay my requests before you and wait in expectation.

Ps 5:1-3 NIV

For I have heard the slander of many: fear was on every side: while they took counsel together against me, they devised to take away my life. But I trusted in thee, O Lord: I said, Thou art my God. My times are in thy hand: deliver me from the hand of mine enemies, and from them that persecute me.

Ps 31:13-15 KJ

Susan Eaves

Blessed are ye, when men shall revile you, and persecute you, and shall say all manner of evil against you falsely, for my sake. Rejoice, and be exceeding glad: for great is your reward in heaven: for so persecuted they the prophets which were before you.

Mt 5:11-12 KJ

Ye that love the Lord hate evil: he preserveth the souls of his saints; he delivereth them out of the hand of the wicked.

Ps 97:10 KJ

SPIRITUAL WARFARE

For by thee I have run through a troop: by my God have I leaped over a wall. As for God, his way is perfect; the word of the Lord is tried: he is a buckler to all them that trust in him.

2 Sam 22:30-31 KJ

The angel of the Lord encampeth round about them that fear him, and delivereth them.

Ps 34:7 KJ

It is God who arms me with strength and makes my way perfect.

2 Sam 22:33 NIV

For thou hast girded me with strength to battle: them that rose up against me hast thou subdued under me.

2 Sam 22:40 KJ

Finally, my brethren, be strong in the Lord, and in the power of his might. Put on the whole armour of God that ye may be able to stand against the wiles of the devil.

Eph 6:10-11 KJ

For our struggle is not against flesh and blood, but against the rulers, against the authorities, against the powers of this dark world and against the spiritual forces of evil in the heavenly realms. Therefore put on the full armor of God, so that when the day of evil comes, you may be able to stand your ground, and after you have done everything, to stand.

Eph 6:12-13 NIV

And take the helmet of salvation, and the sword of the Spirit, which is the word of God.

Eph 6:17 KJ

Stand firm then, with the belt of truth buckled around your waist, with the breastplate of righteousness in place, and with your feet fitted with the readiness that comes from the gospel of peace. In addition to all this, take up the shield of faith, with which you can extinguish all the flaming arrows of the evil one.

Eph 6:14-16 NIV

STRENGTH

Thou wilt keep him in perfect peace, whose mind is stayed on thee: because he trusteth in thee. Trust ye in the Lord forever, for in the Lord Jehovah is everlasting strength.

Isa 26:3-4 KJ

The Lord will give strength unto his people; the Lord will bless his people with peace.

Ps 29:11 KJ

For thou hast girded me with strength to battle: them that rose up against me hast thou subdued under me.

2 Sam 22:40 KJ

In the day when I cried thou answerest me, and strengthenest me with strength in my soul.

Ps 138:3 KJ

I have strength for all things in Christ who empowers me [I am ready for anything and equal to anything through Him Who infuses inner strength into me; I am self-sufficient in Christ's sufficiency].

Phil 4:13AMP

The Lord is my rock, and my fortress, and my deliverer; my God, my strength, in whom I will trust; my buckler, and the horn of my salvation, and my high tower.

Ps 18:2 KJ

For thus saith the Lord God, the Holy One of Israel; In returning and rest shall ye be saved; in quietness and in confidence shall be your strength: and ye would not.

Isa 30:15 KJ

And he said unto me, My grace is sufficient for thee: for my strength is made perfect in weakness.

2 Cor 12:9 KJ

Neither be ye sorry; for the joy of the Lord is your strength.

Neh 8:10 KJ

But the God of all grace, who hath called us unto his eternal glory by Christ Jesus, after that ye have suffered a while, make you perfect, stablish, strengthen, settle you.

1 Pet 5:10 KJ

STRESS

"Lord, help!" they cried in their trouble, and he saved them from their distress. He calmed the storm to a whisper and stilled the waves. What a blessing was that stillness as he brought them safely into harbor!

Ps 107:28-30 NLT

But now thus saith the Lord that created thee, O Jacob, and he that formed thee, O Israel, Fear not: for I have redeemed thee, I have called thee by thy name; thou art mine. When thou passest through the waters, I will be with thee; and through the rivers, they shall not overflow thee: when thou walkest through the fire, thou shalt not be burned; neither shall the flame kindle upon thee.

Isa 43:1-2 KJ

How great is your goodness, which you have stored up for those who fear you, which you bestow in the sight of men on those who take refuge in you. In the shelter of your presence you hide them from the intrigues of men; in your dwelling you keep them safe from accusing tongues.

Ps 31:19-20 NIV

Indeed, the very hairs of your head are all numbered. Don't be afraid; you are worth more than many sparrows.

Lk 12:7 NIV

In righteousness you will be established: Tyranny will be far from you; you will have nothing to fear. Terror will be far removed; it will not come near you. If anyone does attack you, it will not be my doing; whoever attacks you will surrender to you.

Isa 54:14-15 NIV

Get rid of all bitterness, rage, anger, harsh words, and slander, as well as all types of evil behavior. Instead, be kind to each other, tenderhearted, forgiving one another, just as God through Christ has forgiven you.

Eph 4:31-32 NLT

There remaineth therefore a rest to the people of God.

Heb 4:9 KJ

For only we who believe can enter his rest. As for the other, God said, "In my anger I took an oath: 'They will never enter my place of rest'," even though this rest has been ready since he made the world.

Heb 4:3 NLT

The Lord will give strength unto his people; the Lord will bless his people with peace.

Ps 29:11 KJ

STRIFE

Cast out the scorner, and contention shall go out; yea, strife and reproach shall cease.

Pr 22:10 KJ

The discretion of a man deferreth his anger; and it is his glory to pass over a transgression.

Pr 19:11 KJ

Drive out the scoffer, and contention will go out; yes, strife and abuse will cease.

Pr 22:10 AMP

Thou hast delivered me from the strivings of the people; and thou hast made me the head of the heathen: a people whom I have not known shall serve me. It is God that avengeth me and subdueth the people under me. He delivereth me from mine enemies: yea, thou liftest me up above those that rise up against me: thou hast delivered me from the violent man.

Ps 18:43, 47-48 KJ

Drive out the mocker, and out goes strife; quarrels and insults are ended.

Pr 22:10 NIV

I urge you, brothers, to watch out for those who cause divisions and put obstacles in your way that are contrary to the teaching you have learned. Keep away from them. For such people are not serving our Lord Christ, but their own appetites. By smooth talk and flattery they deceive the minds of naive people. Everyone has heard about your obedience, so I am full of joy over you; but I want you to be wise about what is good, and innocent about what is evil. The God of peace will soon crush Satan under your feet. The grace of our Lord Jesus be with you.

Rom 16:17-20 NIV

A fool vents all his feelings, but a wise man holds them back.

Pr 29:11 NKJ

SUFFERING

Then we cried out to the Lord, the God of our fathers, and the Lord heard our voice and saw our misery, toil and oppression. So the Lord brought us out of Egypt with a mighty hand and an outstretched arm, with great terror and with miraculous signs and wonders. He brought us to this place and gave us this land, a land flowing with milk and honey.

Deut 26:7-9 NIV

But those who suffer he delivers in their suffering; he speaks to them in their affliction. He is wooing you from the jaws of distress to a spacious place free from restriction, to the comfort of your table laden with choice food.

Job 36:15-16 NIV

If you are wise, your wisdom will reward you; if you are a mocker, you alone will suffer.

Pr 9:12 NIV

He who puts up security for another will surely suffer, but whoever refuses to strike hands in pledge is safe.

Pr 11:15 NIV

A prudent person foresees danger and takes precautions. The simpleton goes blindly on and suffers the consequences.

Pr 22:3 NLT

He is despised and rejected of men; a man of sorrows, and acquainted with grief: and we hid as it were our faces from him; he was despised, and we esteemed him not. Surely he hath borne our griefs, and carried our sorrows: yet we did esteem him stricken, smitten of God, and afflicted. But he was wounded for our transgressions, he was bruised for our iniquities: the chastisement of our peace was upon him; and with his stripes we are healed.

Isa 53:3-5 KJ

O Lord, thou knowest: remember me, and visit me, and revenge me of my persecutors; take me not away in thy long-suffering: know that for thy sake I have suffered rebuke. Thy words were found, and I did eat them; and thy word was unto me the joy and rejoicing of mine heart: for I am called by thy name, O Lord God of hosts.

Jer 15:15-16 KJ

For just as the sufferings of Christ flow over into our lives, so also through Christ our comfort overflows. If we are distressed, it is for your comfort and salvation; if we are comforted, it is for your comfort, which produces in you patient endurance of the same sufferings we suffer. And our hope for you is firm, because we know that just as you share in our sufferings, so also you share in our comfort.

2 Cor 1:5-7 NIV

TERMINAL ILLNESSES / INCURABLE DISEASES

O Lord my God, I cried to you for help, and you restored my health.

Ps 30:2 NLT

I will delight myself in thy statutes: I will not forget thy word.

Ps 119:16 KJ

He is despised and rejected of men; a man of sorrows, and acquainted with grief: and we hid as it were our faces from him; he was despised, and we esteemed him not. Surely he hath borne our griefs, and carried our sorrows: yet we did esteem him stricken, smitten of God, and afflicted. But he was wounded for our transgressions, he was bruised for our iniquities: the chastisement of our peace was upon him; and with his stripes we are healed.

Isa 53:3-5 KJ

For thus saith the Lord unto the house of Israel, Seek ye me, and ye shall live: But seek not Bethel, nor enter into Gilgal, and pass not to Beersheba: for Gilgal shall surely go into captivity, and Bethel shall come to nought. Seek the Lord, and ye shall live.

Amos 5:4-6 KJ

He brought them out of darkness and the shadow of death, and brake their bands in sunder.

Ps 107:14 KJ

I shall not die, but live, and declare the works of the Lord.

Ps 118:17 KJ

He sent out his word and healed them, snatching them from the door of death.

Ps 107:20 NLT

Thou wilt shew me the path of life: in thy presence is fulness of joy; at thy right hand there are pleasures for evermore.

Ps 16:11 KJ

Thou hast granted me life and favour, and thy visitation hath reserved my spirit.

Job 10:12 KJ

The thief cometh not, but for to steal, and to kill, and to destroy: I am come that they might have life, and that they might have it more abundantly.

Jn 10:10 KJ

THE GOD KIND OF LIFE

The Lord protects those of childlike faith; I was facing death, and he saved me. He has saved me from death, my eyes from tears, my feet from stumbling.

Ps 116:6, 8 NLT

Give ear and come to me; hear me that your soul may live. I will make an everlasting covenant with you, my faithful love promised to David.

Isa 55:3 NIV

"Obey the LORD by doing what I tell you. Then it will go well with you, and your life will be spared."

Jer 38:20 NIV

Nevertheless if thou warn the righteous man, that the righteous sin not, and he doth not sin, he shall surely live, because he is warned; also thou hast delivered thy soul.

Ezek 3:21 KJ

Uphold me according unto thy word, that I may live: and let me not be ashamed of my hope.

Ps 119:116 KJ

Thou wilt shew me the path of life: in thy presence is fulness of joy; at thy right hand there are pleasures for evermore.

Ps 16:11 KJ

A sound heart is the life of the flesh: but envy the rottenness of the bones.

Pr 14:30 KJ

But God is my helper. The Lord keeps me alive!

Ps 54:4 NLT

My enemies did their best to kill me, but the LORD rescued me.

Ps 118:13 NLT

I shall not die, but live, and declare the works of the LORD.

Ps 118:17 NKJ

THE NAME OF THE LORD

For they speak against thee wickedly, and thine enemies take thy name in vain.

Ps 139:20 KJ

Reverencing the name of the Lord brings great blessings but those who take his name in vain are considered his enemies.

Which category are you in?

The Lord hear thee in the day of trouble; the name of the God of Jacob defend thee.

Ps 20:1 KJ

The name of the Lord is a strong tower: the righteous runneth into it, and is safe.

Pr 18:10 KJ

And it shall come to pass, that whosoever shall call on the name of the Lord shall be delivered.

Joel 2:32 KJ

Susan Eaves

Because he hath set his love upon me, therefore will I deliver him: I will set him on high, because he hath known my name.

Ps 91:14 KJ

But unto you that fear my name shall the Sun of righteousness arise with healing in his wings.

Mal 4:2 KJ

For unto us a child is born, unto us a son is given: and the government shall be upon his shoulder: and His name shall be called Wonderful, Counselor, the Mighty God the everlasting Father, the Prince of Peace.

Isa 9:6 KJ

And his name through faith in his name hath made this man strong, whom ye see and know: yea, the faith which is by him hath given him this perfect soundness in the presence of you all.

Acts 3:16 KJ

THE POWER OF A GODLY LIFE

But know that the Lord hath set apart him that is godly for himself: the Lord will hear when I call unto him.

Ps 4:3 KJ

For this shall every one that is godly pray unto thee in a time when thou mayest be found: surely in the floods of great waters they shall not come nigh unto him.

Ps 32:6 KJ

Now we know that God heareth not sinners: but if any man be a worshipper of God, and doeth his will, him he heareth.

Jn 9:31 KJ

For godly sorrow worketh repentance to salvation not to be repented of: but the sorrow of the world worketh death.

2 Cor 7:10 KJ

Oh, the joys of those who do not follow the advice of the wicked, or stand around with sinners, or join in with mockers. But they delight in the law of the Lord, meditating on it day and night.

Ps 1:1-2 NLT

Lord, who shall abide in thy tabernacle? Who shall dwell in thy holy hill? He that walketh uprightly, and worketh righteousness, and speaketh the truth in his heart. He that backbiteth not with his tongue, nor doeth evil to his neighbor, nor taketh up a reproach against his neighbor.

Ps 15:1-3 KJ

The Lord knoweth how to deliver the godly out of temptations, and to reserve the unjust unto the day of judgment to be punished.

2 Pet 2:9 KJ

He that believeth on me, as the scripture hath said, out of his belly shall flow rivers of living water.

Jn 7:38 KJ

For sin shall not have dominion over you: for ye are not under the law, but under grace.

Rom 6:14 KJ

For the kingdom of God is not in word, but in power.

1 Cor 4:20 KJ

THE POWER OF FAITH

Who through faith conquered kingdoms, administered justice, and gained what was promised; who shut the mouths of lions, quenched the fury of the flames, and escaped the edge of the sword; whose weakness was turned to strength; and who became powerful in battle and routed foreign armies.

Heb 11:33-34 NIV

But without faith it is impossible to please him: for he that cometh to God must believe that he is, and that he is a rewarder of them that diligently seek him.

Heb 11:6 KJ

And blessed is she that believed: for there shall be a performance of those things which were told her from the Lord.

Lk 1:45 KJ

For with God nothing shall be impossible.

Lk 1:37 KJ

And Jesus answering saith unto them, Have faith in God. For verily I say unto you, that whosoever shall say unto this mountain, Be thou removed, and be thou cast into the sea; and shall not doubt in his heart, but shall believe that those things which he saith shall come to pass; he shall have whatsoever he saith. Therefore I say unto you, what things soever ye desire, when ye pray, believe that ye receive them, and ye shall have them. And when ye stand praying, forgive, if ye have ought against any: that your Father also which is in heaven may forgive you your trespasses.

Mk 11:22-25 KJ

Cast not away therefore your confidence, which hath great recompence of reward. For ye have need of patience that, after ye have done the will of God, you might receive the promise.

Heb 10:35-36 KJ

Let us hold fast the profession of our faith without wavering; for he is faithful that promised.

Heb 10:23 KJ

Now unto him that is able to do exceeding abundantly above all that we ask or think, according to the power that worketh in us.

Eph 3:20 KJ

For whatsoever is born of God overcometh the world: and this is the victory that overcometh the world, even our faith.

1 Jn 5:4 KJ

And I will give unto thee the keys of the kingdom of heaven: and whatsoever thou shalt bind on earth shall be bound in heaven: and whatsoever thou shalt loose on earth shall be loosed in heaven.

Mt 16:19 KJ

THE POWER OF FORGIVENESS

So shall ye say unto Joseph, Forgive, I pray thee now, the trespass of thy brethren, and their sin; for they did unto thee evil: and now, we pray thee, forgive the trespass of the servants of the God of thy father. And Joseph wept when they spake unto him. And Joseph said unto them, Fear not: for am I in the place of God?

Gen 50:17, 19 KJ

Let the wicked forsake his way, and the unrighteous man his thoughts: and let him return unto the Lord, and he will have mercy upon him; and to our God, for he will abundantly pardon.

Isa 55:7 KJ

A soft answer turneth away wrath: but grievous words stir up anger.

Pr 15:1 KJ

Let all bitterness, and wrath, and anger, and clamour, and evil speaking, be put away from you, with all malice: And be ye kind one to another, tenderhearted, forgiving one another, even as God for Christ's sake hath forgiven you.

Eph 4:31-32 KJ

And when ye stand praying, forgive, if ye have ought against any: that your Father also which is in heaven may forgive you your trespasses. But if ye do not forgive, neither will your Father which is in heaven forgive your trespasses.

Mk 11:25-26 KJ

Dearly beloved, avenge not yourselves, but rather give place unto wrath: for it is written, Vengeance Is mine; I will repay, saith the Lord Therefore if thine enemy hunger, feed him; if he thirst, give him to drink: for in so doing thou shalt heap coals of fire on his head. Be not overcome of evil, but overcome evil with good.

Rom 12:19-21 KJ

Let all bitterness, and wrath, and anger, and clamour, and evil speaking, be put away from you with all malice: And be ye kind one to another, tenderhearted, forgiving one another, even as God for Christ's sake hath forgiven you.

Eph 4:31-32 KJ

If we confess our sins, he is faithful and just to forgive us our sins, and to cleanse us from all unrighteousness.

1 Jn 1:9 KJ

Because thou shalt forget thy misery, and remember it as waters that pass away.

Job 11:16 KJV

THE POWER OF HOPE

Now the God of hope fill you with all joy and peace in believing, that ye may abound in hope, through the power of the Holy Ghost.

Rom 15:13 KJ

Why art thou cast down, O my soul? And why art thou disquieted within me? Hope in God: for I shall yet praise him, who is the health of my countenance, and my God.

Ps 43:5 KJ

You are my refuge and my shield; your word is my source of hope.

Ps 119:114 NLT

Behold, the eye of the Lord is upon them that fear him, upon them that hope in his mercy.

Ps 33:18 KJ

That by two immutable things, in which it was impossible for God to lie, we might have a strong consolation, who have fled for refuge to lay hold upon the hope set before us: Which hope we have as an anchor of the soul, both sure and stedfast, and which entereth into that within the veil.

Heb 6:18-19 KJ

Now the God of hope fill you with all joy and peace in believing, that ye may abound in hope, through the power of the Holy Ghost.

Ro 15:13 KJ

Be of good courage, and he shall strengthen your heart, all ye that hope in the Lord.

Ps 31:24 KJ

Who against hope believed in hope, that he might become the father of many nations, according to that which was spoken, So shall thy seed be.

Ro 4:18 KJ

And hope maketh not ashamed; because the love of God is shed abroad in our hearts by the Holy Ghost which is given unto us.

Ro 5:5 KJ

Now the God of hope fill you with all joy and peace in believing, that ye may abound in hope, through the power of the Holy Ghost.

Ro 15:13 KJ

THE POWER OF OUR WORDS

Death and life are in the power of the tongue; and they that love it shall eat the fruit thereof.

Pr 18:21 KJ

The tongue can bring death or life; those who love to talk will reap the consequences.

Pr 18:21 NLT

I call heaven and earth to record this day against you, that I have set before you life and death, blessing and cursing: therefore choose life, that both thou and thy seed may live.

Deut 30:19 KJ

A gentle tongue [with its healing power] is a tree of life, but willful contrariness in it breaks down the spirit.

Pr 15:4 AMP

Have faith in God. For verily I say unto you, That whosoever shall say unto this mountain, Be thou removed, and be thou cast into the sea; and shall not doubt in his heart, but shall believe that those things which he saith shall come to pass he shall have whatsoever he saith. Therefore I say unto you, what things soever ye desire, when ye pray, believe that ye receive them, and ye shall have them.

Mk 11:22-24 KJ

A good man out of the good treasure of his heart bringeth forth that which is good; an evil man out of the evil treasure of his heart bringeth forth that which is evil: for of the abundance of the heart his mouth speaketh.

Lk 6:45 KJ

A fool's mouth is his destruction, and his lips are the snare of his soul.

Pr 18:7 KJ

Thou shalt also decree a thing, and it shall be established unto thee: and the light shall shine upon thy ways.

Job 22:28 KJ

The mouth of the upright shall deliver them.

Pr 12:6 KJ

He that keepeth his mouth keepeth his life: but he that openeth wide his lips shall have destruction.

Pr 13:3 KJ

Pleasant words are as an honeycomb, sweet to the soul, and health to the bones.

Pr 16:24 KJ

A soft answer turneth away wrath: but grievous words stir up anger.

Pr 15:1 KJ

THE POWER OF PRAYER

If my people, which are called by my name, shall humble themselves, and pray, and seek my face, and turn from their wicked ways; then will I hear from heaven, and will forgive their sin, and will heal their land.

2 Ch 7:14 KJ

Confess your faults one to another, and pray one for another, that ye may be healed. The effectual fervent prayer of a righteous man availeth much.

Ja 5:16 KJ

If I regard iniquity in my heart, the Lord will not hear me: But verily God hath heard me; he hath attended to the voice of my prayer. Blessed be God, which hath not turned away my prayer, nor his mercy from me.

Ps 66:18-20 KJ

Then shalt thou call, and the Lord shall answer; thou shalt cry, and he shall say, Here I am. If thou take away from the midst of thee the yoke, the putting forth of the finger, and speaking vanity;

Isa 58:9 KJ

For I know the thoughts that I think toward you, saith the Lord, thoughts of peace, and not of evil, to give you an expected end. Then shall ye call upon me, and ye shall go and pray unto me, and I will hearken unto you. And ye shall seek me, and find me, when ye shall search for me with all your heart.

Jer 29:11-13 KJ

How the king rejoices in your strength, O Lord! He shouts with joy because you give him victory. For you have given him his heart's desire; you have withheld nothing he requested. He asked you to preserve his life, and you granted his request.

Ps 21:1-2, 4 NLT

When he prays to God, he will be accepted. And God will receive him with joy and restore him to good standing.

Job 33:26 NLT

THE POWER OF RIGHT THINKING

Thy word is a lamp unto my feet, and a light unto my path.

Ps 119:105 KJ

The tongue has the power of life and death, and those who love it will eat its fruit.

Pr 18:21 NIV

The Spirit of the Lord will rest on him— the Spirit of wisdom and of understanding, the Spirit of counsel and of power, the Spirit of knowledge and of the fear of the Lord.

Isa 11:2 NIV

You who are far away, hear what I have done; you who are near, acknowledge my power!

Isa 33:13 NIV

And with all deceivableness of unrighteousness in them that perish; because they received not the love of the truth, that they might be saved.

2 Th 2:10 KJ

I have no greater joy than to hear that my children walk in truth.

3 John 1:4 KJ

And ye shall know the truth, and the truth shall make you free.

Jn 8:32 KJ

Therefore hath the Lord recompensed me according to my righteousness, according to the cleanness of my hands in his eyesight. With the merciful thou wilt shew thyself merciful; with an upright man thou wilt shew thyself upright; With the pure thou wilt shew thyself pure; and with the froward thou wilt shew thyself froward.

Ps 18:24-26 KJ

The law of the Lord is perfect, converting the soul: the testimony of the Lord is sure, making wise the simple. The statutes of the Lord are right, rejoicing the heart: the commandment of the Lord is pure, enlightening the eyes.

Ps 19:7-8 KJ

What man is he that feareth the Lord? him shall he teach in the way that he shall choose.

Ps 25:12 KJ

The meek will he guide in judgment: and the meek will he teach his way.

Ps 25:9 KJ

And thine ears shall hear a word behind thee, saying, This is the way, walk ye in it, when ye turn to the right hand, and when ye turn to the left.

Isa 30:21 KJ

THE POWER OF THE CROSS

Who has believed our report? And to whom has the arm of the Lord been revealed? For He shall grow up before Him as a tender plant, And as a root out of dry ground. He has no form or comeliness; And when we see Him, There is no beauty that we should desire Him. He is despised and rejected by men. A man of sorrows and acquainted with grief. And we hid, as it were, our faces from Him; He was despised, and we did not esteem Him. Surely He has borne our griefs and carried our sorrows; Yet we esteemed Him stricken, Smitten by God, and afflicted. But He was wounded for our transgressions; He was bruised for our iniquities: The chastisement for our peace was upon Him, And by His stripes we are healed. All we like sheep have gone astray; We have turned, every one, to his own way; And the Lord has laid on Him the iniquity of us all.

Isa 53:1-6 NKJ

And you, being dead in your trespasses and the uncircumcision of you flesh, He has made alive together with Him, having forgiven you all trespasses, having wiped out the handwriting of requirements that was against us, which was contrary to us. And He has taken it out of the way, having nailed it to the cross. Having disarmed principalities and powers, He made a public spectacle of them, triumphing over them in it.

Col 2:13-15 NKJ

We do this by keeping our eyes on Jesus, the champion who initiates and perfects our faith. Because of the joy awaiting Him, He endured the cross, disregarding its shame. Now He is seated in the place of honor beside God's throne.

Heb 12:2 NLT

If you confess with your mouth the Lord Jesus and believe in your heart that God has raised Him from the dead, you will be saved. For with the heart one believes unto righteousness, and with the mouth confession is made unto salvation.

Rom 10:9-10 KJ

Which none of the princes of this world knew: for had thy known it, they would not have crucified the Lord of glory. But as it is written, Eye hath not seen, nor ear heard, neither have entered into the heart of man, the things which God hath prepared for them that love Him.

1 Cor 2:8-9 KJ

And being found in fashion as a man, He humbled himself, and became obedient unto death, even the death of the cross. Wherefore God also hath highly exalted Him, and given Him a name which is above every name. That at the name of Jesus every knee should bow, of things in heaven, and things in earth, and things under the earth.

Phil 2:8-10 KJ

For the preaching of the cross is to them that perish foolishness; but unto us which are saved it is the power of God.

1 Cor 2:18 KJ

For His is our peace, who hath made both one, and hath broken down the middle wall of partition between us; Having abolished in His flesh the enmity, even the law of commandments contained in ordinances; for to make in Himself of twain one new man, so making peace; And that He might reconcile both unto God in one body by the cross, having slain the enmity thereby.

Eph 2:14-16 KJ

Christ has redeemed us from the curse of the law, having become a curse for us (for it is written, Cursed is everyone who hangs on a tree) that the blessing of Abraham might come upon the Gentiles in Christ Jesus, that we might receive the promise of the Spirit through faith.

Gal 3:13-14 NKJ

THREATS

The engulfing waters threatened me, the deep surrounded me; seaweed was wrapped around my head. To the roots of the mountains I sank down; the earth beneath barred me in forever. But you brought my life up from the pit, O Lord my God. When my life was ebbing away, I remembered you, Lord, and my prayer rose to you, to your holy temple.

Jn 2:5-7 NIV

And now, Lord, behold their threatenings: and grant unto thy servants, that with all boldness they may speak thy word.

Acts 4:29 KJ

When they hurled their insults at him, he did not retaliate; when he suffered, he made no threats. Instead, he entrusted himself to him who judges justly.

1 Pet 2:23 NIV

The Lord is good, a strong hold in the day of trouble; and he knoweth them that trust in him.

Na 1:7 KJ

Blessed be God, even the Father of our Lord Jesus Christ, the Father of mercies, and the God of all comfort; Who comforteth us in all our tribulation, that we may be able to comfort them which are in any trouble, by the comfort wherewith we ourselves are comforted of God.

2 Co 1:3-4 KJ

His enemies will not defeat him, nor will the wicked overpower him. I will beat down his adversaries before him and destroy those who hate him. My faithfulness and unfailing love will be with him and by my authority he will grow in power.

Ps 89:22-24 NLT

How long will you people ruin my reputation? How long will you make groundless accusations? How long will you continue your lies? You can be sure of this: the Lord set apart the godly for himself. The Lord will answer when I call to him.

Ps 4:2-3 KJ

A thousand shall fall at thy side, and ten thousand at thy right hand; but it shall not come nigh thee.

Ps 91:7 KJ

TRAGEDY

The Spirit of the Lord God is upon me; because the Lord hath anointed me to preach good tidings unto the meek; he hath sent me to bind up the brokenhearted, to proclaim liberty to the captives, and the opening of the prison to them that are bound; To proclaim the acceptable year of the Lord, and the day of vengeance of our God; to comfort all that mourn; To appoint unto them that mourn in Zion, to give unto them beauty for ashes, the oil of joy for mourning, the garment of praise for the spirit of heaviness.

Isa 61:1-3 KJ

The Lord cares deeply when his loved ones die.

Ps 116:15 NLT

In that day the people will proclaim, "This is our God! We trusted in him, and he saved us! This is the Lord, in whom we trusted. Let us rejoice in the salvation he brings!"

Isa 25:9 NLT

I will be glad and rejoice in thy mercy: for thou hast considered my trouble; thou hast known my soul in adversities.

Ps 31:7 KJ

Give your burdens to the Lord, and he will take care of you. He will not permit the godly to slip and fall.

Ps 55:22 NLT

When they walk through the Valley of Weeping, it will become a place of refreshing springs. The autumn rains will clothe it with blessings.

Ps 84:6-7 NLB

But thou, O Lord, art a shield for me; my glory, and the lifter up of mine head.

Ps 3:3 KJ

He tends his flock like a shepherd: He gathers the lambs in his arms and carries them close to his heart; he gently leads those that have young.

Isa 40:11 NIV

On the day the Lord gives you relief from suffering and turmoil and cruel bondage, you will take up this taunt against the king of Babylon: How the oppressor has come to an end! How his fury has ended!

Isa 14:3-4 NIV

TROUBLE

The Lord is good, a refuge in times of trouble. He cares for those who trust in him.

Nah 1:7 NIV

No weapon that is formed against thee shall prosper; and every tongue that shall rise against thee in judgment thou shalt condemn. This is the heritage of the servants of the Lord, and their righteousness is of me, saith the Lord.

Isa 54:17 KJ

I will be glad and rejoice in your unfailing love, for you have seen my troubles, and you care about the anguish of my soul. You have not handed me over to my enemies but have set me in a safe place.

Ps 31:7-8 NLT

He shall call upon me, and I will answer him: I will be with him in trouble; I will deliver him, and honour him.

Ps 91:15 KJ

So we take comfort and are encouraged and confidently and boldly say, The Lord is my Helper; I will not be seized with alarm [I will not fear or dread or be terrified]. What can man do to me?

Heb 13:6 AMP

Casting the whole of your care [all your anxieties, all your worries, all your concerns, once and for all] on Him, for He cares for you affectionately and cares about you watchfully.

1 Pet 5:7 AMP

Let not your heart be troubled: ye believe in God, believe also in me.

Jn 14:1 KJ

Surely every man walks to and fro--like a shadow in a panto-mime; surely for futility and emptiness he is in turmoil; each one heaps up riches, not knowing who will gather them. And now, Lord, what do I wait for and expect? My hope and expec-tation are in You.

Ps 39:6-7 AMP

Moreover I will appoint a place for my people Israel, and will plant them, that they may dwell in a place of their own, and move no more; neither shall the children of wickedness afflict them any more, as beforetime.

2 Sam 7:10 KJ

Peace I leave with you, my peace I give unto you: not as the world giveth, give I unto you. Let not your heart be troubled, neither let it be afraid.

Jn 14:27 KJ

UNCERTAINTY

Being confident of this, that he who began a good work in you will carry it on to completion until the day of Christ Jesus.

Phil 1:6 NIV

Susan Eaves

And without faith it is impossible to please God, because anyone who comes to him must believe that he exists and that he rewards those who earnestly seek him.

Heb 11:6 NIV

And we have the word of the prophets made more certain, and you will do well to pay attention to it, as to a light shining in a dark place, until the day dawns and the morning star rises in your hearts.

2 Pet 1:19 NIV

But be sure to fear the Lord and serve him faithfully with all your heart; consider what great things he has done for you.

1 Sam 12:24 NIV

For lack of guidance a nation falls, but many advisers make victory sure.

Pr 11:14 NIV

God is not unjust; he will not forget your work and the love you have shown him as you have helped his people and continue to help them. We want each of you to show this same diligence to the very end, in order to make your hope sure.

Heb 6:10-11 NIV

For I will pour water upon him that is thirsty, and floods upon the dry ground: I will pour my spirit upon thy seed, and my blessing upon thine offspring.

Isa 44:3 KJ

Men ought always to pray and not to faint.

Lk 18:1 KJ

But know that the Lord hath set apart him that is godly for himself: the Lord will hear when I call unto him.

Ps 4:3 KJ

The Lord preserveth the simple: I was brought low, and he helped me.

Ps 116:6 KJ

UNFAIR CIRCUMSTANCES

Don't envy violent people or copy their ways. Such wicked people are detestable to the Lord, but he offers his friendship to the godly.

Pr 3:31-32 NLT

Day by day the Lord takes care of the innocent, and they will receive an inheritance that lasts forever. They will not be disgraced in hard times; even in famine they will have more than enough.

Ps 37:18-19 NLT

He delivereth the poor in his affliction, and openeth their ears in oppression.

Job 36:15 KJ

In all their affliction he was afflicted, and the angel of his presence saved them: in his love and in his pity he redeemed them; and he bare them, and carried them all the days of old.

Isa 63:9 KJ

Let all bitterness, and wrath, and anger, and clamour, and evil speaking, be put away from you, with all malice.

Eph 4:31 KJ

Have not I commanded thee? Be strong and of a good courage, be not afraid, neither be thou dismayed: for the Lord thy God is with thee whithersoever thou goest.

Josh 1:9 KJ

For the Lord shall be thy confidence, and shall keep thy foot from being taken.

Pr 3:26 KJ

VERBAL ABUSE

I come to you for protection, O Lord my God. Save me from my persecutors - rescue me! If you don't, they will maul me like a lion, tearing me to pieces with no one to rescue me. Arise, O Lord, in anger! Stand up against the fury of my enemies! Wake up, my God, and bring justice!

Ps 7:1-2, 6 NLT

The Lord replies, "I have seen violence done to the helpless, and I have heard the groans of the poor. Now I will rise up to rescue them, as they have longed for me to do."

Ps 12:5 NLT

Great peace have they who love your law, nothing can make them stumble.

Ps 119:165 NIV

As for God, his way is perfect; the word of the Lord is tried: he is a buckler to all them that trust in him.

2 Sam 22:31 KJ

And let us arise, and go up to Bethel; and I will make there an altar unto God, who answered me in the day of my distress, and was with me in the way which I went.

Gen 35:3 KJ

Blessed be God, even the Father of our Lord Jesus Christ, the Father of mercies, and the God of all comfort; Who comforteth us in all our tribulation, that we may be able to comfort them which are in any trouble, by the comfort wherewith we ourselves are comforted of God. For as the sufferings of Christ abound in us, so our consolation also aboundeth by Christ.

2 Cor 1:3-5 KJ

For the Lord shall comfort Zion: he will comfort all her waste places; and he will make her wilderness like Eden, and her desert like the garden of the Lord; joy and gladness shall be found therein, thanksgiving, and the voice of melody.

Isa 51:3 KJ

Give me a sign of your goodness, that my enemies may see it and be put to shame, for you, O Lord, have helped me and comforted me.

Ps 86:17 NIV

Susan Eaves

VICTORY

And such as do wickedly against the covenant shall he corrupt by flatteries: but the people that do know their God shall be strong, and do exploits.

Dan 11:32 KJ

It wasn't their swords that took the land. It wasn't their power that gave them victory. But it was your great power and strength. You were with them because you loved them.

Ps 44:3 NCV

You saved us from our foes, and you made our enemies ashamed.

Ps 44:7 NCV

Now thanks be unto God, which always causeth us to triumph in Christ, and maketh manifest the savour of his knowledge by us in every place.

2 Cor 2:14 KJ

Oh, what joy for those whose disobedience is forgiven, whose sin is put out of sight!

Ps 32:1 NLT

The Lord gave David victory wherever he went.

2 Sam 8:6 NIV

It was not by their sword that they won the land, nor did their arm bring them victory; it was your right hand, your arm, and the light of your face, for you loved them. You are my King and my God, who decrees victories for Jacob.

Ps 44:3-4 NIV

But thou hast saved us from our enemies, and hast put them to shame that hated us.

Ps 44:7 KJ

WEAKNESS

I will search for my lost ones who strayed away, and I will bring them safely home again. I will bandage the injured and strengthen the weak.

Ezek 34:16 NLT

Beat your plowshares into swords and your pruninghooks into spears: let the weak say, I am strong.

Joel 3:10 KJ

But God hath chosen the foolish things of the world to confound the wise; and God hath chosen the weak things of the world to confound the things which are mighty;

1 Cor 1:27 KJ

He sent his word and healed them, and delivered them from their destructions.

Ps 107:20 KJ

But you belong to God, my dear children. You have already won a victory over those people, because the Spirit who lives in you is greater than the spirit who lives in the world.

1 Jn 4:4 NLT

Each time he said, "My grace is all you need. My power works best in weakness." So now I am glad to boast about my weaknesses, so that the power of Christ can work through me. That's why I take pleasure in my weaknesses, and in the insults, hardships, persecutions, and troubles that I suffer for Christ. For when I am weak, then I am strong.

2 Cor 12:9-10 NLT

O spare me, that I may recover strength, before I go hence, and be no more.

Ps 39:13 KJ

The Lord is my light and my salvation so why should I be afraid? The Lord is my fortress, protecting me from danger, so why should I tremble?

Ps 27:1 NLT

He feels pity for the weak and the needy, and he will rescue them.

Ps 72:13 NLT

WEARINESS

Then he answered and spake unto me, saying, This is the word of the Lord unto Zerubbabel, saying, Not by might, nor by power, but by my spirit, saith the Lord of hosts.

Zech 4:6 KJ

To appoint unto them that mourn in Zion, to give unto them beauty for ashes, the oil of joy for mourning, the garment of praise for the spirit of heaviness; that they might be called trees of righteousness, the planting of the Lord, that he might be glorified.

Isa 61:3 KJ

I long to obey your commandments! Renew my life with your goodness.

Ps 119:40 NLT

O Lord, oppose those who oppose me. Fight those who fight against me.

Ps 35:1 NLT

As for God, his way is perfect; the word of the Lord is tried: he is a buckler to all them that trust in him.

2 Sam 22:31 KJ

Behold, I will do a new thing; now it shall spring forth; shall ye not know it? I will even make a way in the wilderness, and rivers in the desert.

Isa 43:19 KJ

Susan Eaves

O Lord, you are so good, so ready to forgive, so full of unfailing love for all who ask for your help.

Ps 86:5 NLT

With this news, strengthen those who have tired hands, and encourage those who have weak knees. Say to those with fearful hearts, "Be strong, and do not fear, for your God is coming to destroy your enemies. His is coming to save you."

Isa 35:3-4 NLT

WHAT GOD WANTS YOU TO RECEIVE

But as many as received him, to them gave he power to become the sons of God, even to them that believe on his name.

Jn 1:12 KJ

Jesus said unto her, I am the resurrection, and the life: he that believeth in me, though he were dead, yet shall he live: And whosoever liveth and believeth in me shall never die. Believest thou this?

Jn 11:25-26 KJ

To open their eyes, and to turn them from darkness to light, and from the power of Satan unto God, that they may receive forgiveness of sins, and inheritance among them which are sanctified by faith that is in me.

Acts 26:18 KJ

For thus saith the LORD unto the house of Israel, Seek ye me, and ye shall live.

Amos 5:4 KJ

And by knowledge shall the chambers be filled with all precious and pleasant riches. A wise man is strong; yea, a man of knowledge increaseth strength.

Pr 24:4-5 KJ

He who leads the upright along an evil path will fall into his own trap, but the blameless will receive a good inheritance.

Pr 28:10 NIV

The blind receive their sight, and the lame walk, the lepers are cleansed, and the deaf hear, the dead are raised up, and the poor have the gospel preached to them.

Matt 11:5 KJ

For if, by the trespass of the one man, death reigned through that one man, how much more will those who receive God's abundant provision of grace and of the gift of righteousness reign in life through the one man, Jesus Christ.

Rom 5:17 NIV

For your shame ye shall have double; and for confusion they shall rejoice in their portion: therefore in their land they shall possess the double: everlasting joy shall be unto them.

Isa 61:7 KJ

And every one that hath forsaken houses, or brethren, or sisters, or father, or mother, or wife, or children, or lands, for my name's sake, shall receive an hundredfold, and shall inherit everlasting life.

Matt 19:29 KJ

Let us then approach the throne of grace with confidence, so that we may receive mercy and find grace to help us in our time of need.

Heb 4:16 NIV

Jesus answered and said unto them, Verily I say unto you, If ye have faith, and doubt not, ye shall not only do this which is done to the fig tree, but also if ye shall say unto this mountain, Be thou removed, and be thou cast into the sea; it shall be done.

Matt 21:21 KJ

As God's fellow workers we urge you not to receive God's grace in vain. For he says, "In the time of my favor I heard you, and in the day of salvation I helped you." I tell you, now is the time of God's favor, now is the day of salvation.

2 Cor 6:1-2 NIV

Verily I say unto you, whosoever shall not receive the kingdom of God as a little child, he shall not enter therein.

Mark 10:15 KJ

For that very reason I was shown mercy so that in me, the worst of sinners, Christ Jesus might display his unlimited patience as an example for those who would believe on him and receive eternal life.

1 Tm 1:16 NIV

And Jesus answering saith unto them, Have faith in God. For verily I say unto you, that whosoever shall say unto this mountain, Be thou removed, and be thou cast into the sea; and shall not doubt in his heart, but shall believe that those things which he saith shall come to pass; he shall have whatsoever he saith. Therefore I say unto you, what things soever ye desire, when ye pray, believe that ye receive them, and ye shall have them. And when ye stand praying, forgive, if ye have ought against any: that your Father also which is in heaven may forgive you your trespasses. But if ye do not forgive, neither will your Father which is in heaven forgive your trespasses.

Mark 11:22-26 KJ

Jesus stopped and ordered the man to be brought to him. When he came near, Jesus asked him, "What do you want me to do for you?" "Lord, I want to see," he replied.

Luke 18:40-41 NIV

Christ hath redeemed us from the curse of the law, being made a curse for us: for it is written, Cursed is every one that hangeth on a tree: That the blessing of Abraham might come on the Gentiles through Jesus Christ; that we might receive the promise of the Spirit through faith.

Gal 3:13-14 KJ

But ye shall receive power, after that the Holy Ghost is come upon you: and ye shall be witnesses unto me both in Jerusalem, and in all Judaea, and in Samaria, and unto the uttermost part of the earth.

Acts 1:8 KJ

Cast not away therefore your confidence, which hath great recompence of reward. For ye have need of patience, that, after ye have done the will of God, ye might receive the promise.

Heb 10:35-36 KJ

Blessed is the man that endureth temptation: for when he is tried, he shall receive the crown of life, which the Lord hath promised to them that love him.

James 1:12 KJ

Hitherto have ye asked nothing in my name: ask, and ye shall receive, that your joy may be full.

Jn 16:24 KJ

WHEN IT SEEMS LIKE YOUR FAITH IS FAILING

Be careful for nothing; but in every thing by prayer and supplication with thanksgiving let your requests be made known unto God. And the peace of God, which passeth all understanding, shall keep your hearts and minds through Christ Jesus.

Phil 4:6-7 KJ

The Lord hear thee in the day of trouble; the name of the God of Jacob defend thee.

Ps 20:1 KJ

So then faith cometh by hearing, and hearing by the word of God.

Rom 10:17 KJ

That the communication of thy faith may become effectual by the acknowledging of every good thing which is in you in Christ Jesus.

Phm 1:6 KJ

Being confident of this very thing, that he which hath begun a good work in you will perform it until the day of Jesus Christ.

Phil 1:6 KJ

Now faith is the substance of things hoped for, the evidence of things not seen.

Heb 11:1 KJ

That your faith should not stand in the wisdom of men, but in the power of God.

1 Cor 2:5 KJ

O Lord, I have come to you for protection: don't let me be disgraced.

Ps 71:1 NLT

For whatsoever is born of God overcometh the world: and this is the victory that overcometh the world, even our faith.

1 Jn 5:4 KJ

WHEN YOU ARE
EMOTIONALLY DRAINED

The high and lofty one who lives in eternity, the Holy One, says this: I live in the high and holy place with those whose spirits are contrite and humble. I restore the crushed spirit of the humble and revive the courage of those with repentant hearts.

Isa 57:15 NLT

For thou wilt not leave my soul in hell; neither wilt thou suffer thine Holy One to see corruption.

Ps 16:10 KJ

Bring my soul out of prison, that I may praise thy name: the righteous shall compass me about; for thou shalt deal bountifully with me.

Ps 142:7 KJ

The Lord protects those of childlike faith; I was facing death, and he saved me. Let my soul be at rest again, for the Lord has been good to me.

Ps 116:6-7 NLT

There has no temptation taken you but such as is common to man; but God is faithful, who will not suffer you to be tempted above that ye are able; but will with the temptation also make a way to escape, that ye may be able to bear it.

1 Cor 10:13 KJ

And let us not be weary in well doing; for in due season we shall reap, if we faint not.

Gal 5:1 KJ

If we believe not, yet he abideth faithful: he cannot deny himself.

2 Tim 2:13 KJ

Stay alert! Watch out for your great enemy, the devil. He prowls around like a roaring lion looking for someone to devour. Stand firm against him, and be strong in your faith. Remember that your Christian brothers and sisters all over the world are going though the same kind of suffering you are.

1 Pet 5:8-9 NLT

WHEN YOU ARE WOUNDED

I will give you back your health and heal your wounds, says the Lord.

Jer 30:17 NLT

The Lord will comfort Israel again and have pity on her ruins. Her desert will blossom like Eden, her barren wilderness like the garden of the Lord. Joy and gladness will be found there. Songs of thanksgiving will fill the air.

Isa 51:3 NLT

But he was pierced for our rebellion, crushed for our sins. He was beaten so we could be whole. He was whipped so we could be healed.

Isa 53:5 NLT

He heals the brokenhearted and bandages their wounds.

Ps 147:3 NLT

Feel my pain and see my trouble. Forgive all my sins.

Ps 25:18 NLT

I am sick at heart. How long, O Lord, until you restore me? Return, O Lord, and rescue me. Save me because of your unfailing love. The Lord has heard my plea; the Lord will answer my prayer.

Ps 6:3-4, 9 NLT

And it shall come to pass in the day that the Lord shall give thee rest from thy sorrow, and from thy fear, and from the hard bondage wherein thou wast made to serve.

Isa 14:3 KJ

Then he said unto them, Go your way, eat the fat, and drink the sweet, and send portions unto them for whom nothing is prepared: for this day is holy unto our Lord: neither be ye sorry; for the joy of the Lord is your strength.

Neh 8:10 KJ

WHEN YOU HAVE
BLOWN IT

Some were fools; they rebelled and suffered for their sins. They couldn't stand the thought of food, and they were knocking on death's door. "Lord, help!" they cried in their trouble, and he saved them from their distress. He sent out his word and healed them, snatching them from the door of death.

Ps 107:17-20 NLT

If he did this for fools how much more his own children?

But if the wicked will turn from all his sins that he hath committed, and keep all my statutes, and do that which is lawful and right, he shall surely live, he shall not die. All his transgressions that he hath committed, they shall not be mentioned unto him: in his righteousness that he hath done he shall live.

Ezek 18:21-22 KJ

If he would do this for the wicked how much more for his children?

They reel to and fro, and stagger like a drunken man, and are at their wit's end. Then they cry unto the Lord in their trouble, and he bringeth them out of their distresses. He maketh the storm a calm, so that the waves thereof are still.

Ps 107:27-29 KJ

Some sat in darkness and deepest gloom, imprisoned in iron chains of misery. They rebelled against the words of God, scorning the counsel of the Most High. That is why he broke them with hard labor; they fell, and no one was there to help them. "Lord, help!" they cried in their trouble, and he saved them from their distress. He led them from the darkness and deepest gloom; he snapped their chains. Let them praise the Lord for his great love and for the wonderful things he has done for them.

Ps 107:10-15 KJ

You have spoken in my hearing, and I have heard your very words

Job 33:8 NLT

He hath not dealt with us after our sins; nor rewarded us according to our iniquities. For as the heaven is high above the earth, so great is his mercy toward them that fear him. As far as the east is from the west, so far hath he removed our transgressions from us.

Ps 103:10-12 KJ

WHEN YOU NEED HELP
FROM HEAVEN

Do what is good and run from evil so that you may live! Then the Lord God of Heaven's Armies will be your helper, just as you have claimed.

Amos 5:14 NLT

O Israel: who is like unto thee, O people saved by the Lord, the shield of thy help, and who is the sword of thy excellency! And thine enemies shall be found liars unto thee; and thou shalt tread upon their high places.

Deut 33:29 KJ

Lord, it is nothing with thee to help, whether with many, or with them that have no power: help us, O Lord our God; for we rest on thee, and in thy name we go against this multitude. O Lord, thou art our God; let no man prevail against thee.

2 Chr 14:11 KJ

Be strong and courageous! Don't be afraid or discouraged because of the king of Assyria or his mighty army, for there is a power far greater on our side! He may have a great army, but they are merely men. We have the Lord our God to help us and to fight our battles for us!" Hezekiah's words greatly encouraged the people.

2 Chr 32:7-8 NLT

But in my distress I cried out to the Lord; yes, I prayed to my God for help. He heard me from his sanctuary; my cry to him reached his ears.

Ps 18:6 NLT

He will rescue the poor when they cry to him; he will help the oppressed, who have no one to defend them.

Ps 72:12 KJ

The Lord preserveth the simple: I was brought low, and he helped me.

Ps 116:6 KJ

And it came to pass in process of time, that the king of Egypt died: and the children of Israel sighed by reason of the bondage, and they cried, and their cry came up unto God by reason of the bondage. And God heard their groaning, and God remembered his covenant with Abraham, with Isaac, and with Jacob.

Ex 2:23-24 KJ

WHEN YOU'RE AWAY FROM GOD

I will search for my lost ones who strayed away, and I will bring them safely home again. I will bandage the injured and strengthen the weak.

Ezek 34:16 NLT

Wherewithal shall a young man cleanse his way? by taking heed thereto according to thy word.

Ps 119:9 KJ

I used to wander off until you disciplined me; but now I closely follow your word.

Ps 119:67 NLT

I have gone astray like a lost sheep; seek thy servant; for I do not forget thy commandments.

Ps 119:176 KJ

Seeing then that we have a great high priest, that is passed into the heavens, Jesus the Son of God, let us hold fast our profession.

Heb 4:14 KJ

Wherefore I say unto thee, Her sins, which are many, are forgiven; for she loved much: but to whom little is forgiven, the same loveth little.

Lk 7:47 KJ

Oh, what joy for those whose disobedience is forgiven, whose sin is put out of sight! When I refused to confess my sin, my body wasted away, and I groaned all day long.

Ps 32:1, 3 NLT

For I will declare mine iniquity; I will be sorry for my sin.

Ps 38:18 KJ

WHEN YOUR SOUL IS SICK

For thou wilt not leave my soul in hell; neither wilt thou suffer thine Holy One to see corruption.

Ps 16:10 KJ

Bring my soul out of prison, that I may praise thy name: the righteous shall compass me about; for thou shalt deal bountifully with me.

Ps 142:7 KJ

He restoreth my soul: he leadeth me in the paths of righteousness for his name's sake.

Ps 23:3 KJ

Return unto thy rest, O my soul; for the Lord hath dealt bountifully with thee. For thou hast delivered my soul from death, mine eyes from tears, and my feet from falling.

Ps 116:7-8 KJ

O Lord, truly I am thy servant; I am thy servant, and the son of thine handmaid: thou hast loosed my bonds.

Ps 116:16 KJ

So we don't look at the troubles we can see now; rather, we fix our gaze on things that cannot be seen. For the things we see now will soon be gone, but the things we cannot see will last forever.

2 Cor 4:18 NLT

When I remember these things, I pour out my soul in me: for I had gone with the multitude, I went with them to the house of God, with the voice of joy and praise, with a multitude that kept holyday.

Ps 42:4 KJ

My soul melteth for heaviness: strengthen thou me according unto thy word.

Ps 119:28 KJ

Yea, his soul draweth near unto the grave, and his life to the destroyers. If there be a messenger with him, an interpreter, one among a thousand, to shew unto man his uprightness: Then he is gracious unto him, and saith, Deliver him from going down to the pit: I have found a ransom. His flesh shall be fresher than a child's: he shall return to the days of his youth: He shall pray unto God, and he will be favorable unto him: and he shall see his face with joy: for he will render unto man his righteousness.

Job 33:22-26 KJ

My soul melteth for heaviness: strengthen thou me according unto thy word.

Ps 119:28 KJ

Many there be which say of my soul, There is no help for him in God. Selah. But thou, O Lord, art a shield for me; my glory, and the lifter up of mine head.

Ps 3:2-3 KJ

O Lord, truly I am thy servant; I am thy servant, and the son of thine handmaid: thou hast loosed my bonds.

Ps 116:16 KJ

So we don't look at the troubles we can see now; rather, we fix our gaze on things that cannot be seen. For the things we see now will soon be gone, but the things we cannot see will last forever.

2 Co 4:18 NLT

WISDOM

If any of you lack wisdom, let him ask of God, that giveth to all men liberally, and upbraideth not; and it shall be given him.

Ja 1:5 KJ

The fear of the Lord is the beginning of wisdom: a good understanding have all they that do his commandments.

Ps 111:10 KJ

And God gave Solomon wisdom and understanding exceeding much, and largeness of heart, even as the sand that is on the seashore.

1 Kings 4:29 KJ

God said to Solomon, "Since this is your heart's desire and you have not asked for wealth, riches or honor, nor for the death of your enemies, and since you have not asked for a long life but for wisdom and knowledge to govern my people over whom I have made you king, therefore wisdom and knowledge will be given you. And I will also give you wealth, riches and honor, such as no king who was before you ever had and none after you will have."

2 Chr 1:11-12 NIV

For the Lord giveth wisdom: out of his mouth cometh knowledge and understanding. He layeth up sound wisdom for the righteous: he is a buckler to them that walk uprightly.

Pr 2:6-7 KJ

The fear of the Lord is the beginning of wisdom, and knowledge of the Holy One is understanding.

Pr 9:10 NIV

Thou shalt guide me with thy counsel.

Ps 73:24 KJ

Wisdom is the principal thing; therefore get wisdom: and with all thy getting get understanding. Exalt her, and she shall promote thee: she shall bring thee to honour, when thou dost embrace her.

Pr 4:7-8 KJ

I have taught thee in the way of wisdom; I have led thee in right paths. When thou goest, thy steps shall not be straitened; and when thou runnest, thou shalt not stumble. Take fast hold of instruction; let her not go: for she is thy life.

Pr 4:11-13 KJ

WORRY

I am leaving you with a gift—peace of mind and heart. And the peace I give is a gift the world cannot give. So don't be troubled or afraid.

Jn 14:27 NLT

O our God, won't you stop them? We are powerless against this mighty army that is about to attack us. We do not know what to do, but we are looking to you for help.

2 Chr 20:12 NLT

The fear of the Lord is the beginning of knowledge: but fools despise wisdom and instruction.

Pr 1:7 KJ

But all who listen to me will live in peace, untroubled by fear of harm.

Pr 1:33 NLT

The oath which he sware to our father Abraham. That he would grant unto us that we being delivered out of the hand of our enemies might serve him without fear.

Lk 1:73-74 KJ

Say to those with fearful hearts, "Be strong, and do not fear, for your God is coming to destroy your enemies. He is coming to save you."

Isa 35:4 NLT

Don't be afraid, for I am with you. Don't be discouraged, for I am your God. I will strengthen you and help you. I will hold you up with my victorious right hand.

Isa 41:10 NLT

You will look in vain for those who tried to conquer you. Those who attack you will come to nothing. For I hold you by your right hand- I, the Lord your God. And I say to you, 'Don't be afraid, I am here to help you'.

Isa 41:12-13 NLT

The Lord shall give thee rest from your sorrow, and from your fear and the hard bondage in which you were made to serve.

Isa 14:3 KJ

TO RECEIVE
ETERNAL LIFE

Behold, I stand at the door, and knock: if any man hear my voice, and open the door, I will come in to him, and will sup with him, and he with me.

Heb 3:20 KJ

That if thou shalt confess with thy mouth the Lord Jesus, and shalt believe in thine heart that God hath raised him from the dead, thou shalt he saved. For with the mouth man believes unto righteousness; and with the mouth confession is made unto salvation.

Ho 10:9-10 KJ

Jesus, I believe You died for my sins, I believe You rose from the dead. I confess You as my Lord and Savior. Please come into my life and make me Your child. I confess my sins to You. Help me to know what is pleasing to You. Give me the power to turn away from all sin. I promise to live my life for You. Thank you for writing my name in the Lamb's Book of Life. In Jesus' name, Amen.

If you've prayed this prayer for the first time, let someone else know. If you've rededicated your life to the Lord, know He is the God of a second chance. His Word tells us His mercies are new every morning. Please write to me and let me know. I encourage you to join a local church that believes the Bible is the Word of God. Ask the Lord to direct your steps. He won't disappoint you!

SUSAN EAVES

Inspirational Keynote Speaker

Susan Eaves is a teacher, author and personal growth coach. Her life has been described as truly inspiring. She has overcome panic attacks, severe depression, tragedy and a heart-breaking past. She teaches with joy, compassion, humor and mesmerizing motivation.

Is your group or organization looking for someone that can captivate an audience with life-changing insights and real life examples? Susan inspires people from all walks of life with God-given strategies that work! She shares the life-changing principles that God taught her in the valley. These principles changed her life and have helped change the lives of many others.

For over twenty-three years she has taught her life enrichment principles at business conferences, seminars, and churches internationally. Susan has been a guest on a multitude of television and radio shows. Her passion is people. Her message - God can turn around the most desperate, unfair, hopeless, heart-breaking circumstances and bring destiny and purpose to them.

Be inspired as Susan shares how to overcome toxic thinking, recover from tragedy and devastation, and go on to lead a fulfilling and victorious life.

IN SUSAN'S OWN WORDS

I know that God has put me here to help others come out of devastation and to break the cycles of hopelessness and defeat. What God has done in my life, He wants to do in the lives of others. My assignment and joy is to show others how…

A Sample of Susan's Life Changing Topics

Give God One Year, Transform Your Life Forever
Rediscovering Purpose after Life-Shattering Events
Defeating Toxic Thinking
Overcoming Adversity
Triumphing over Panic Attacks, Anxiety and Stress
Victory over Depression
Forgiving the Impossible

For contact or additional information visit our websites.
susaneaves.com
thecrisisbible.com
theiambook.com

Or write us at:

Good Fellas Publishing
P.O. Box 7
Osprey, FL 34229

If this book has been a blessing to you, we would be honored if you would tell others about it.

Part of the proceeds from this book will go to benefit children worldwide.

Give *The Crisis Topical Bible* as a gift of hope. These are difficult and challenging times that we are living in. People need to know where to turn in crisis. You may never know what this gift given in someone's greatest hour of need may do for them.

We are open to suggestions on places where you would like to see *The Crisis Topical Bible* sold such as: bookstores, churches, organizations and anywhere else you conduct business. Your input is greatly appreciated!

We give group discounts, purchase gift copies.

Recommend *The Crisis Topical Bible* on your Facebook, Blog, Twitter, Myspace or any other outlet or media you have access to.

Ask your local supermarket, bookstore, hospital, AA group or rehab facility to purchase it.

Use *The Crisis Topical Bible* for a fundraising event at your local charity, club, school or civic organization.

Contact us at:
susaneaves.com
thecrisistopicalbible.com
theiambook.com

Or Write us at:
Good Fellas Publishing
P.O. Box 7
Osprey, FL 34229

Made in United States
North Haven, CT
14 May 2022